WHEN STAYING

The Cost of Holding on Too Long!

JACQUELINE MOSS

Attention: Permissions Coordinator
Welcome To The Storm Publishing!
info@w2tspublishing.org

Ordering Information:
Quantity sales. Special discounts are available on quantity purchases by corporations, associations, and others. For details, contact the publisher at the email address above.

Orders by U.S. trade bookstores and wholesalers.

Library of Congress Control Number: 2025910417

ISBN: 978-1-966612-24-7

Cover Design: Amir N. of mir_grafics

Veronica Miller, Red Diamond Editing by V. Rena,
reddiamondediting5@yahoo.com

First Printed Edition: June 2025

Printed in the United States of America

CONTENTS

From My Heart to Yours

This book isn't written out of anger—it is written out of healing. Out of truth. Out of love. It is written for every woman who stayed too long, for every child who silently carried what they weren't meant to hold, and for every mother who believed she had to break herself just to keep her family whole.

I didn't always know I would tell this story. For years, I held it inside. Covered it up with busyness, buried it under titles—Mom, Wife, Nurse, Strong One. But eventually, the weight of silence grew heavier than the truth itself. And when I began to speak, I found freedom. And I found purpose.

This story isn't about revenge. It's not about painting someone as a villain. It's about finally honoring the voice I silenced for too long—and honoring the many women who've done the same. It's about my children, too—the ones who lived in the tension of love and dysfunction and never stopped loving me through it all.

So, if you're reading this and see pieces of yourself, know that this isn't just my story—it's *ours*.

"He heals the brokenhearted and binds up their wounds." —Psalm 147:3

Let this book be part of your healing. Let these pages remind you that you're not alone. And let my journey light the way for your own.

With love,

Jacqueline

Introduction

I used to believe that staying was the best thing I could do for my children. I told myself that, no matter what, they deserved a two-parent home—something I never had growing up. I convinced myself that my love, my sacrifice, and my endurance would be enough to give them stability. That it would protect them from the pain of a broken family.

But what I didn't realize—what I was too deep in the struggle to see—was that staying wasn't saving them. It was shaping them. And not in the way I had hoped.

For over two decades, I remained in a relationship that drained me, convinced that my children would be better off seeing their parents together. I believed I was doing the right thing by holding on—for them. But what I failed to see at the time was that they were watching everything. Not just the moments when we laughed as a family, but the moments when I was silent when I should have spoken up. The moments when I stayed when I should have walked away. And now, years later, I can see the effects of my choice.

My three oldest children—the ones who grew up watching me endure—are now walking some of the same paths I did. They've found themselves in relationships where they stay, even when it hurts, because that's what they saw me do. They're holding on, no matter the cost, because that's what I modeled for them.

But my two youngest daughters—who were still young when I finally made the decision to leave—see relationships differently. They don't carry the same pressure to stay at all costs. They understand that love should never mean losing yourself, because they saw a different version of me—a woman who finally chose herself.

This book is not about blame. It's not about regret. It's about awareness.

It's about understanding how our choices as parents shape the way our children view love, relationships, and self-worth. It's about realizing that sometimes, staying for the sake of the kids can do more harm than good. And it's about breaking the cycle—because it's never too late to show our children a new way.

If you've ever stayed in a relationship longer than you should have, or if you've ever convinced yourself that enduring was the best thing for your children, I want you to know, you're not alone. But I also want you to know this:

Sometimes, leaving isn't just about saving yourself. Sometimes, it's about saving them, too. This is my story. My truth. And the lessons I learned the hard way. Because when staying hurts, the cost is higher than we ever imagined.

CHAPTER 1
The Absence That Shaped Me

I can still remember the family gatherings at my grandparents' home—laughter filling the air, the smell of fish frying outside, and the warmth of togetherness. These moments were supposed to be joyful, and in many ways, they were. But for me, they were also a reminder of what my family was missing.

Surrounded by my cousins, I noticed something: they all had both parents. Their fathers were there, grilling, playing games, or just sitting with their wives, enjoying the day. And then there was my family—just my mother, carrying the weight of both roles. She was our mother and our father, doing everything she could to make sure we never felt the void. But I could see it in her eyes. I could see the exhaustion, the silent struggle, the longing for something more.

Even though my mother loved us deeply, we still felt the absence of a father. Life in a single-parent home wasn't easy. We struggled financially, emotionally, and mentally. My mother carried the burden alone, and I understood—even as a child—how much harder life was without the presence of a father in the home.

But what hit the hardest wasn't just our struggle—it was watching what we lacked reflected in the lives of those around us.

Among all my relatives, there was one person I looked up to the most—my aunt. She had everything I thought a family should have. She was married, had six children—three boys and three girls—just like the family I dreamed of having one day. Their household was full of love and support, and most importantly, they had God at the center of their lives. I admired her deeply, not just because of how she carried herself, but because of the life she had built.

Growing up alongside my cousins and going to church with them on Sundays, I spent a lot of time with them. They were intelligent, well-mannered, and always seemed to have a sense of security that I longed for. Their father had a great job, and from the outside looking in, they never seemed to struggle the way we did. I saw their family as stable, loving, and complete—everything I wished for myself. And in my young mind, I convinced myself that this—a father in the home, a stable household, a life with structure—was the key to happiness. The solution to all of life's problems.

It was in those moments, watching my aunt and her family, that I made a promise to myself: when I had children, they would grow up in a two-parent home. I would create the stability I never had. I would make sure they never felt the void that I did. No matter what, I would not let them experience the struggles I faced growing up.

But my reality turned out different.

One of the biggest struggles I witnessed with my mother was when we had to move out of our home and stay with my uncle and his family. I was about nine years old when we left, and we didn't move out until I was around twelve. My mother, my sister, and I had to share one small room, sleeping in the same bed every night. It wasn't just an adjustment—it was a harsh reality that life wasn't stable for us. Having to leave our home to move in with family was difficult, not just because of the crowded space, but because it was a reminder that we didn't have the security others seemed to take for granted.

I saw how hard it was for my mother to navigate that situation—how much she carried on her shoulders alone. Watching her struggle made me even more determined. More than ever, I knew that when I had children, I would do everything in my power to provide them with the stability I never had. I wanted them to feel secure, to know they could rely on both parents, and to never question whether they were truly loved.

At the time, I believed that love meant holding a family together, no matter what. I thought that as long as two parents were under the same roof, children would be okay. I thought that struggle didn't matter as long as we stayed together. I had no idea that the desire for stability, if placed above all else, could come at a cost.

But here's what I've learned since: you can't heal childhood wounds by sacrificing your adulthood. You can't fix the past by bleeding into the future.

My father's absence shaped me—but it didn't define me. It taught me how to mother with a full heart, how to love without condition, and how to fight even when I was tired. But it also taught me the importance of healing. Of choosing peace over patterns. Of becoming the parent, I needed—not just for my children, but for the little girl inside me who still sometimes aches for what she didn't get.

This was the beginning. Not because of my pain but because of my purpose. And even though it took years to see that clearly, I know now that the absence didn't break me.

It built me.

Section 2
How His Absence Shaped My Views on Love & Relationships

As a child, my father's absence felt like a personal rejection. I couldn't understand why he wasn't there. Was I not good enough? Why did he leave us to build a life with someone else—a woman he married, a new family he chose? I convinced myself that he had forgotten about me, that I didn't matter to him. I didn't feel loved by him—not in the way a little girl should feel loved by her daddy.

I would see him once, maybe twice a year, always around Christmas like clockwork—just enough to remind me of what I didn't have the rest of the year. Those visits were short and awkward. He'd show up, exchange gifts, maybe smile for a few photos, and then be gone again. And each time he left, it felt like he took a piece of me with him.

Whenever I asked my mama where he was or why he wasn't around, she'd just say, "He went into the army." That was the extent of it. Eventually, she told me he got out, got married, and had another child. They were living in Connecticut, and that was that. It was a lot to carry as a child—to know he had chosen to build a new life, a new family, somewhere else.

One of the only things that made me feel connected to him was the time I spent with my grandma, Dora—his mother. I got to be with her during some holidays and summer breaks. She was a quiet, strong woman, and being in her home brought a certain kind of comfort. I remember how she got up early to cook breakfast—homemade biscuits with molasses or cheese, rice and sausage, and sometimes even fried fish. That kitchen smelled like love. We'd go to yard sales together, sometimes go fishing, and she always had the Sunday obituaries playing on the radio in the background. Those moments with her helped fill in the blanks of the family I wished I had.

But even with all that warmth, I couldn't shake the ache I felt when I saw my father with his wife and their daughter. Seeing them together stirred something deep inside me. Why did she get the pretty clothes, the attention, the money—the life that felt so far out of reach for me? Why was my mama struggling just to keep food on the table while they looked like they had everything? Why was I not being cared for and treated the same way she was? I was heartbroken. I felt *abandoned*—as if I had been left behind while he moved forward with his new family.

That abandonment shaped my deepest convictions. I told myself, over and over again, that I would only have children by one man. I didn't want my children to feel this brokenness—to grow up wondering why they weren't enough. I didn't want them to have to compete with half-siblings or to feel like they were second-best. I wanted them to know, without question, that they were loved. That they belonged.

Growing up without my father's presence was more than just emotional, it was *a struggle* in every sense of the word. We lived on welfare, barely making ends meet. My mother did the best she could, but there was never enough. Clothes were handed down until they were too worn to wear. I remember washing our clothes in a bucket, hanging them by the wooden stove or the kerosene heater just to get them dry. The smell that clung to them afterward was awful, and it made me self-conscious.

At school, I was teased and bullied—reminded, over and over, that I was different. That I was lacking.

The days I went to school in smelly clothes, I felt humiliation like never before. I was embarrassed. Ashamed. A failure. Less than. I wanted to disappear—to be invisible so no one would notice me. Some days, I just wanted to be alone. Other days, I wanted to fit in like the regular kids at school—to play sports, go to school dances, just be normal. But those things weren't in the cards for me. That life—the carefree childhood that I longed for—never happened.

Instead, I made a vow to myself: *I would be better than my mother.* I would do things differently. I would create a better life for me and my future family. I would make sure my children never knew the kind of pain, struggle, and humiliation that I had endured.

Still today, I tell my children that their lives—their choices—should be better than the life I created for them. They should build something stronger. Something healthier. They should break the cycle.

At the time, I convinced myself that the answer was simple: as long as the family stayed together, everything would be okay. A two-parent home meant security. It meant never feeling the pain of being unwanted. It meant protection from the hardships I had faced. I equated love with stability, believing that as long as someone stayed, it meant they cared. I never wanted to experience abandonment again, and I feared that leaving—even from an unhealthy situation—would mirror what my father had done to me.

I clung to that belief because it gave me hope. It gave me a vision of a future that felt safe.

I didn't know then that staying together, no matter what, could come with its own set of consequences. But that was something I would come to understand much later.

Section 3
The Search for Stability

To be honest, when I met my ex-husband, I wasn't looking for love. I was sixteen years old, just trying to focus on building a future for myself at Atlanta Job Corps. He was twenty-two. I had a boyfriend back home—he was incarcerated at the time—but I was still holding it down, staying loyal despite everything.

One weekend, my best friend invited me to hang out with her and her boyfriend. She told me his brother was coming to pick us up and that I should come along. That brother rolled up to Job Corps in this big, loud, yellow station wagon. He was older, cool, and had that confident energy that made you pay attention—even when you didn't mean to.

Since I rarely went out on weekends, I figured, why not? It was just supposed to be a night to unwind, to dance, to laugh, and to feel young for a moment. We drank a little, partied, and had fun. But looking back, I realize I didn't really know what love was back then. I had never seen it modeled in a healthy way. All I knew was what I lacked—and I mistook attention for affection and comfort for connection. Then everything changed. I got pregnant.

That moment shifted everything. Suddenly, life wasn't just about me anymore. Every decision I made from that point on would affect someone else—someone who hadn't even arrived yet. I remember thinking, *"This is it. This is my chance to create the kind of family I always wanted."* A full family. A real family. But my excitement was tangled up with fear, uncertainty, and a desperate hope that somehow, this would all come together.

By the time I found out I was pregnant, I had completed my GED and earned my Certified Nursing Assistant (CNA) certification at Job Corps. That's also where I met my child's father- the brother who rolled up to Job Corps one day in a big yellow station wagon, like he owned the place. We started talking, and before long, he became the center of my world. So, I made the decision to go back home and tell my mom. Here I was, sixteen—about to turn seventeen—and carrying life. I sat her down and told her I was pregnant and that I was going back to Atlanta to be with my child's father.

Because deep in my heart, I believed I could give my child something I never had—*a father*. That dream meant everything to me.

But I didn't have money for a bus ticket. So, I went to work in the fields with my mom, picking butter beans. They paid five dollars a bushel. *Five dollars.* That was backbreaking work in the southern heat, but I did it—day after day, for weeks. My hands were blistered and sore, but I kept going. I was determined to earn enough for that Greyhound ticket. And after nearly two months, I finally had enough to go back.

But even as I packed my bags and planned my return, I started noticing little things that didn't sit right. Days went by without hearing from him. I couldn't always reach him. He didn't know the exact day I was coming back. Something about it all felt off, but I brushed it aside. I told myself he was just busy. That I was overthinking. That everything would be fine once I got there.

When I finally arrived in Atlanta, I had to take a taxi to his house. I remember sitting in the back seat, staring out the window, trying to quiet the knot in my stomach. I should've been excited. But instead, all I felt was this uneasy silence inside me—a sinking feeling I couldn't explain. I was nervous. I was hopeful. But I was also scared.

And in that moment, somewhere between the highway and his doorstep, I started questioning everything. *Why am I the one chasing this dream? Why am I doing all the work? Why does this feel so one-sided?*

But I silenced those doubts. I buried them deep. Because I wanted this to work so badly. I had already told myself that this was my chance to build the family I never had—and I clung to that hope like my life depended on it. Even though, deep down, a quiet voice inside me already knew. I was holding onto something that wasn't holding onto me.

Section 4
Realizing I Was Repeating the Past

The very first time I felt like I was truly trapped in my situation was around four months into my pregnancy. I had spent my last dime on a Greyhound ticket, determined to get back to Atlanta and be with my child's father. I believed I was doing the right thing—choosing family, choosing stability, choosing love.

When I arrived, I paid for a taxi with the little cash I had left. The house door was unlocked, so I walked right in and headed to the bedroom we had once shared. But nothing could've prepared me for what I saw next. He was in bed with another woman.

Not just any woman, but someone I knew from Job Corps. We weren't close, but we were friendly. And I knew he had talked to her before he ever started anything with me. Still, seeing her there—in our bed—was a betrayal that left me hollow. In that moment, it was like the air was sucked from the room. My heart dropped, my body froze, and my spirit felt like it left my body. I just stood there, stunned, barely able to breathe, staring at the scene in front of me.

I had given up everything. My home, my pride, my last dollar—to be with this man. And this is what I walked into?

I should've left right then. But I didn't. Instead, he had me move into the bedroom next door to the one we had once shared. I was placed in a room with another woman—his roommate, or so I thought. Over time, we became friendly. We talked. We shared space. And then one day, I found out the truth—she had been sleeping with him, too.

Still, I stayed. I told myself it was temporary. That things would get better. That none of these women meant anything to him. I held onto the fantasy that once the baby came, everything would fall into place.

For months, I lived in that house, repeating a twisted routine. During the week, I was the girlfriend—the one cooking meals, playing house, pretending everything was okay. But come the weekend, the other woman showed up and slept in my bed—the bed I once called mine. I laid in the next room, pregnant and alone, while he gave her what he promised me.

I buried my rage, swallowed my pride, and convinced myself that my love, my loyalty, my sacrifice would eventually be enough. But then came the breaking point.

I was in the guest room, trying to assemble our baby's crib. My belly was growing, and so was the weight of everything I had endured. I remember how hard it was to screw the pieces together through the tears. I was exhausted—not just physically, but emotionally and spiritually. I had finally reached my limit.

I gave him an ultimatum: her or me. I told him I couldn't do it anymore—not like this, not while carrying his child. His answer wasn't in words. It was *violence*. He picked up one of the side rails from the crib and beat me with it.

That night, I called his mother and his sister to come and get me. I couldn't take it anymore. I left and moved in with his mother, thinking I had finally escaped. For a while, I believed that maybe I was free.

But when his family left the country for a while, they didn't want me to be alone in the final months of my pregnancy. And so, they asked him to stay with me—to "help." Just like that, he was back in my space. Back in my life. And slowly, without even realizing it, I was pulled right back into the cycle I had tried to run from. And that was just the beginning.

Over the next twenty-five years, I endured more betrayal than most can imagine. There was constant cheating, verbal and physical abuse, drug use, financial neglect—even a child born outside our marriage. The emotional and mental abuse ran deep. I had every reason to leave, and yet—I stayed.

I stayed because I thought it was the right thing to do. Because I thought love meant *endurance*. Because I thought my children needed both of their parents. I stayed because I wanted to give them what I never had—a two-parent home. Even if it meant sacrificing my own happiness... and my own safety.

Section 5
The Belief That Kept Me Stuck

Looking back, I can see how my father's absence shaped my entire outlook on love and relationships. I clung to the belief that keeping a family together—no matter the cost—was the key to providing my children with the stability I had never known. That belief ran so deep, I ignored every red flag, every warning sign, every moment that told me I was repeating a painful cycle.

I thought if I could just endure the hardships—if I loved hard enough, fought long enough, and sacrificed enough of myself—I could create the family I had always dreamed of. A family that looked nothing like the one I came from.

But instead of building a home filled with love and safety, I found myself trapped in a relationship that drained me—emotionally, mentally, and physically. The years passed, and with every betrayal, every sacrifice I made in the name of "keeping the peace," I lost more and more of myself.

I told myself I was staying for my children. But if I'm honest, I was also staying because I was afraid—afraid of failing, of being alone, of confirming the deep-down fear that maybe I wasn't good enough after all.

For twenty-five years, I lived a life I never envisioned. Infidelity, abuse, financial struggle, and heartbreak became my normal. I silenced my own needs, convinced that as long as the family stayed together, that meant success. That meant love. That meant I had won.

But what I didn't realize was this: **staying in a broken relationship wasn't giving my children stability**—it was teaching them that *love is supposed to hurt*. That pain and commitment go hand in hand. That sacrificing yourself was what it meant to be part of a family.

I thought I had created the family I always wanted.

But what I really created was a version of stability built on fear. The fear of being alone, the fear of repeating my past, the fear of not being enough. That fear didn't just shape my life. It shaped theirs, too.

CHAPTER 2
When Staying Hurts

For years, I had convinced myself that my life was building toward something greater—that everything I endured growing up had prepared me to create the kind of family I had always dreamed of. And for a brief moment, I thought I had finally done it.

It was 1995, and I was pregnant with our third child—just weeks away from giving birth. At only twenty-one years old, I had already spent years chasing after stability, and for the first time, it felt like we were getting there. My children's father had finally gotten a real job—his first in over five years. That one job allowed him to do something he'd never done before: buy a home.

That home was supposed to be the start of everything we had been working toward—security, stability, family. After all the years we'd spent on welfare, living in the Capitol Homes projects of Atlanta, this house felt like a turning point. A reward for everything I had endured. A sign that maybe—just maybe—the worst was behind us.

I remember when we first moved into the projects in 1992. It was supposed to just be me, pregnant with our second child, and my daughter. We were placed in a one-bedroom apartment. But somehow, our one-bedroom turned into a full house. I moved him in—my children's father.

Then my mama. Then my sister. My mama and sister made a pallet on the floor of the living room each night. There was barely any space, but we made it work. We didn't have much, but we had each other. I remember it like it was yesterday.

So, when we finally got that house in 1995, it felt like we had made it. I still remember walking through that front door for the first time, my hand resting on my belly, thinking—*we're finally going to be okay*. For once, it seemed like he was trying. Like he wanted to be the man I needed him to be. I thought this was it—the moment we became a real family.

But the best part? The look on my children's faces.

In the projects, I had always been cautious—nervous every time they stepped outside. There was violence, drugs, and chaos right outside our front door. I had to watch them like a hawk just to keep them safe. But now? They had a yard. A backyard. Space to run. To be free. To just be kids. Hearing their laughter as they played outside made me feel like I had done something right. Like maybe all the pain had been worth it.

For that moment, I truly believed this was the reason I stayed. This was what I had fought for all those years. I told myself again and again: *I'm doing this for my kids. They deserve a home. They deserve both parents. They deserve a stable life.*

But the truth was... that house wasn't the stability I thought it was.

Because within just one month, the illusion of our happy family began to fall apart.

Section 2
The Reality of Stability

It happened in a way I should've seen coming. For years, I had brushed off the signs, made excuses, and convinced myself that things would eventually get better. But reality doesn't wait for permission to show up. It arrives uninvited—loud, raw, and undeniable.

It was late, and I was standing in our cramped laundry area, doing what I always did—trying to keep the house running, keeping the clothes clean, keeping everything looking normal. I was tired, heavy with pregnancy, my back aching from the weight of everything—literally and emotionally.

I reached into the pockets of his work pants before tossing them into the wash. It was a habit by then. Sometimes I'd find loose change, receipts, lighters, nothing unusual. But that night, I felt something hard and smooth—longer than a lighter, heavier than change. I pulled it out. And there it was. A crack pipe.

My fingers tightened around it, and for a second, I just stared. The room went still. I couldn't move. Couldn't blink. My breath caught in my throat, and I felt a wave of heat rush up my neck. I was holding it in my bare hand like it was burning me—as if letting go would mean letting the whole truth crash down around me.

My heart started pounding so hard I could feel it in my ears. *This can't be real. Not after everything we've been through. Not now.* I walked straight to him, hands shaking, the pipe clenched in my fist.

He didn't even flinch. He looked me in the eyes and lied without missing a beat.

"It's not mine," he said. "I was holding it for a friend."

And as ridiculous as that sounded, a part of me still wanted to believe it. I stood there, searching his face for any trace of the truth—but I already knew. Deep in my gut, I knew. The signs had been there all along. All those late nights, all the times he said he was working overtime. What if he wasn't working at all?

That night, the pieces started snapping together like a puzzle I didn't want to finish. I started replaying every moment, every excuse I had let slide. And then the phone call came. His supervisor, saying that "He hasn't been to work in over a week."

I sat down after that call, the phone still in my hand, and let the truth settle in like a weight on my chest. I had believed he was finally stepping up—finally becoming a provider, a partner, a father. But it was all a lie.

The home, the job, the promises—they weren't rooted in anything real. The stability I thought we had. It was nothing but smoke.

I should've packed my bags that night. I should've walked away. But I didn't. Because I was still holding onto a dream. Still chasing the version of family, I had always longed for. Still convincing myself that if I just held on a little longer, he might change. *We* might make it.

Section 3
When Staying Stopped Feeling Safe

For years, I told myself that keeping the family together was what mattered most. That as long as we were under the same roof, my kids would be okay. I believed that their safety and happiness came from presence—his presence—even if it was dysfunctional. But 1995 began to unravel that belief.

The first time I saw the impact my decisions were having on my children was when their father started disappearing for days at a time. What started as an occasional night out turned into full weekends. Then three, four, sometimes even five days with no explanation. Just gone. And my children noticed.

"Where's Daddy? Why is he gone so much? Did we do something wrong?"

Their questions hit harder than any argument we had. They looked at me with wide, confused eyes, hoping I could make sense of the silence. I didn't have the heart to tell them the truth—that he was out doing God knows what, possibly with a woman our age, possibly with the child he was rumored to have fathered behind my back. They didn't know about the drugs, or the lies, or the double life he was leading while I stayed home trying to keep their world from falling apart. All they knew was Daddy was gone. And Mama was tired.

I did everything I could to keep our lives moving forward. I worked two jobs. Days as a Medical Assistant at Emory University and nights as a Security Officer at Wells Fargo. I barely slept. I barely ate. Some nights, I'd find an empty room during a shift and steal ten minutes of sleep on the floor, just to keep going.

I was running on fumes—physically, emotionally, spiritually. Then the violence escalated.

I had managed to buy a car—finally, something to make life easier. I didn't tell him. I wanted something of my own, something that didn't require his permission or approval. But when he found out, he snapped.

We were standing outside, in front of his dad's friend's house where the car was parked on the street. The air felt heavy, thick with tension. I remember trying to walk away, not wanting to argue, not wanting to cause a scene. But he followed, yelling—accusing me of being sneaky, selfish, dishonest.

Then in a rage, he grabbed me and threw me over the hood of the car. My body slammed against the metal. I hit the pavement hard, my hands instinctively bracing my fall, scraping across the asphalt. The pain didn't come right away—but the blood did.

I looked down and saw my fingernails had been ripped clean off. Raw, red skin throbbed where they used to be. I stared at my hands, dazed, trying to understand how I had ended up here, again. And still, I stayed.

That moment, bloody and broken on the street, should have been my turning point. But it wasn't. Because I had convinced myself that leaving meant breaking my family. That if I walked away, I was failing my children. That if I stayed, somehow, I was still giving them something I never had. But I was wrong.

What I didn't understand then was that I was teaching my children that love looked like chaos. That being a family meant swallowing pain. That staying, no matter the cost, was noble—even when it was destroying me.

Section 4
The Moment I Finally Left

Then came the day I almost lost everything. It was late in the afternoon, the end of my shift at Emory—around 4:30 PM. I was tired, emotionally drained from holding everything together at work and home. I had just taken off my gloves and was about to clock out when my phone rang. The school's number flashed across the screen, and instantly, my heart skipped.

I answered quickly, thinking maybe one of the kids had gotten sick. But the voice on the other end was firm, detached.

"Ms. Harrell, your children have not been picked up from school. If someone doesn't get them within the next thirty minutes, we'll have no choice but to contact social services for child abandonment."

The words hit me like a brick to the chest.

Child Abandonment.

I froze, trying to process what I was hearing. Then the panic set in. My hands trembled as I gripped the phone tighter. I called him—over and over—but he didn't answer. Not once. No explanation. No heads-up. He had simply forgotten our children—lost in a high from smoking crack.

I didn't even clock out. I dropped everything and ran out the side door of the doctor's office, still in my scrubs. The air hit me hard—thick and humid—and I bolted toward the MARTA bus stop. My chest was pounding. I felt like I couldn't breathe.

I sat on the edge of the plastic bus seat, bouncing my leg the entire ride, heart in my throat. Every red light, every stop along the way felt like it was stealing time.

All I could think was, *Please don't let them take my babies. Please let me make it in time.*

By the time I got to the school, the front office was quiet. My babies were sitting there—my daughter with her backpack on her lap, my son fidgeting in his chair—their eyes darting around, confused.

When they saw me, they stood up quickly, relief washing over their faces.

"Mama, where were you?"

And that question shattered me.

I knelt down and pulled them into my arms, right there in the middle of that cold tile floor. I could barely speak past the lump in my throat. They were safe—but I realized just how close I had come to losing them.

And not because I was a bad mother. But because I had been trying to hold together a family that wasn't holding me.

That moment broke something in me—and built something new in its place.

Shortly after, my job at Emory announced they were offering severance packages. I had two choices: transfer or walk away.

I didn't hesitate. I chose to walk away.

I packed up our clothes—just enough for a week—and shoved them into the trunk and front seat of my car. The rest—furniture, toys, photos—I put in storage. It was too much to carry, and honestly, I didn't want the memories weighing us down.

My babies were 4, 7, and 8 years old. They climbed into the backseat, holding on to their blankets and each other. I remember glancing at them through the rearview mirror, their eyes wide but quiet, like they knew this moment mattered, too.

And this time, I didn't look back. I didn't cry. I didn't second guess it. I just drove. Because I knew finally that staying had nearly cost me everything. And leaving? Leaving was saving us.

When Leaving Still Didn't Mean Letting Go

When I left Atlanta, I told myself it was final. I had done the hardest thing I swore for years I'd never do. I had walked away. Not just for me, but for my kids. I had packed up our lives and driven off with only what we could carry, determined never to look back.

But less than two weeks later, I found myself back in that same city—not because I missed him, not because I had regrets, but because I needed to get the rest of our things out of storage. Clothes. Kitchen items. Toys for the kids. The pieces of a life I had left behind in a rush.

We were staying with my mother at the time, squeezed into her tiny two-bedroom single wide mobile home. She had already given up her own bed, choosing to sleep on the couch so my three children and I could have her room. Clothes were folded in laundry baskets. Toys were tucked under the bed. We were making do, but I knew we needed more of our things.

So, I made the drive back to Atlanta with one goal—get in, get the boxes, and get out. No detours. No drama. And definitely no contact with him. But when I pulled up to the storage unit, my stomach turned.

There he was—leaning against the metal door like he'd been waiting. His body was slumped, his eyes glassy. He was high. Clearly high. His legs barely held him up. His face was hollow, and his clothes hung off his frame like they didn't belong to him anymore.

I didn't get out of the car right away. I just sat there, gripping the steering wheel, watching him through the windshield. My chest tightened. My jaw clenched.

And then came the wave—not anger, not hate. But sadness. Guilt. Embarrassment. That familiar tug-of-war between what I knew and what I wished.

He looked nothing like the man I had once fallen for. But he was *still* the father of my children. *Still* the man I had once believed in. And now, he looked like a ghost.

I didn't owe him anything—I knew that. I had left for a reason. But as I sat in the car, I started questioning myself. What kind of mother would I be if I just left him here like this? What if he overdosed? What would I tell the kids? Would they blame me? Would I blame myself?

I knew it wasn't my job to save him. But part of me still hoped—if I could just get him away from the drugs, away from the people who fed his habits... maybe, just maybe, he'd change. Maybe without the streets, the chaos, the distractions—he could finally become the man and father I had always wanted him to be.

So, despite everything I had been through, despite everything I had overcome to leave, I opened the car door and told him to get in. And just like that, I brought him back to North Carolina with me.

Looking back now, I see that I wasn't just going back for the boxes—I was still carrying the weight of believing I could fix him. I didn't understand then that love alone doesn't save someone who isn't ready to be saved. I thought compassion meant sacrifice, and that sacrifice meant staying. But what I didn't know was that by bringing him with me, I wasn't rescuing him—I was reopening the very door I had fought so hard to close.

A Crowded Home and a Second Chance

When I walked through the door with him, my mother and sister just stared. Their faces said everything they didn't need to speak. They had supported me when I left him. They had rearranged their lives, given up comfort, opened their home—and now, here I was, walking back in with the very man they had watched me walk away from.

My mama's expression was tight. Tired. Not angry, but disappointed in the kind of way that made me feel ten years old again. My sister didn't say much, but her silence was loud.

The only ones smiling were my children.

For them, Daddy was back. That was all that mattered. They ran to him, hugged his legs, and pulled at his arms. They didn't know about the broken promises. They didn't know about the drugs. They didn't know about the fear I swallowed every day just trying to keep things together. All they saw was their father—home.

But the truth was, home was already stretched thin. There were seven of us now—me, him, our three kids, my mom, and my sister—all squeezed into a two-bedroom single wide trailer. There wasn't an inch of space that wasn't filled with bodies, bags, blankets, or noise.

For the next two or three months, the five of us—him, me, and the kids—slept in my mom's bedroom. All of us. In her bed. There were nights I'd lie flat on my back, barely able to move, one child on my arm, another curled at my feet, and him beside me, all of us tangled in heat and tension.

I told myself it was temporary. Just a season. Another sacrifice on the way to stability. I kept saying, "We're going to get on our feet again. This is just a bump in the road. But deep down, I was suffocating."

There was no privacy. No peace. No relief. Just noise, pressure, and the weight of trying to pretend like this wasn't unraveling all over again.

Eventually, we moved in with my cousin and his family. It gave us a little more room, but it still wasn't ours. We were still sleeping on someone else's couch or bed, living out of duffle bags, waiting for life to start—again.

And then, just as I was trying to settle into that new, chaotic normal. I found out I was pregnant. Again. I stared at the test in the bathroom, holding it in my hand like it might disappear if I blinked hard enough. I felt like the walls were closing in. My heart was beating fast, my palms sweating, and all I could think was—How am I going to do this?

There was no celebration. No excitement. Just a deep, exhausted silence inside of me. I wasn't even done healing from the last chapter, and here I was, already writing the next one. I didn't say it out loud, but I felt it: This wasn't the fresh start I thought it would be. It was the same cycle, just in a different zip code.

The "Good Years" That Made Me Stay Even Longer

Despite how things had started, the first five years in North Carolina were actually good. It felt strange to admit that after everything we'd been through. But for once, the chaos slowed down. The yelling stopped. The nights wondering where he was stopped. And with it, the deep ache I had grown so used to carrying started to fade—just a little.

The abuse stopped. The drugs stopped, aside from the occasional marijuana, which I told myself wasn't a big deal. After everything else I'd seen him do, a little weed seemed manageable.

The cheating? That seemed to stop, too, or at least there were no obvious signs. And I let myself believe it. He was coming home every night. He'd help with the kids, cook dinner, and fold laundry. I remember coming home to the smell of curry chicken, rice and peas, and fried plantains. He'd sing or rap while stirring the pot, acting like a real family man. And honestly? For a while, it felt real.

After over a decade of cheating, lies, betrayal, and empty promises, I finally felt like I had won. It wasn't perfect, but it was peaceful.

Even though his work wasn't steady, he was doing odd jobs—yard work, helping friends with construction, moving furniture, just enough to bring in a little money. It wasn't enough to support us completely, but he was trying. And after everything we had been through, trying felt like a victory. For the first time in years, I could finally exhale. I could finally focus on me.

In 2000, I was accepted into nursing school. I still remember opening the acceptance letter, holding it like it was a golden ticket. I hadn't been a student in years, and part of me wondered if I still had the discipline, the focus, the confidence to do it. But I showed up. I stayed up late studying flashcards, quizzing myself on medications and anatomy at the kitchen table while the kids slept.

When I graduated with my LPN diploma, it felt like a rebirth. I walked across that stage for every version of me who had put herself last—who had survived abuse, heartbreak, and motherhood while carrying the weight of someone else's addiction.

I got my first job as an LPN at a urologist's office. It wasn't glamorous, but it was mine. My own name tag. My own paycheck. I wasn't just depending on him. I wasn't depending on public assistance either. After 12 years of government help, I finally walked away from it. I remember sitting in the car after submitting the paperwork and crying—not from sadness, but from sheer, exhausted relief.

And because things were going so well between us, in 2003, we did something I never thought I'd do—we got married. Just a simple courthouse ceremony, just the kids, and that ever-persistent hope that maybe we had finally made it.

Then in 2004, we had our fifth child. A beautiful baby girl with a head full of dark curls and the sweetest eyes I'd ever seen. I held her in my arms and thought, *Maybe this is it. Maybe this is finally our happy ending.*

For the first time in a long time, I wasn't just surviving—I was living. And that's why I stayed even longer. Because I had seen the worst in him, and now I was finally getting to see what I thought was the best.

The Reality of Raising Five Kids and Pursuing a Dream

Growing up, I used to look at my aunt like she was a superhero. She had six kids—three girls and three boys—and somehow, she made it look easy. Her house was always full of noise, laughter, and the kind of togetherness I longed for. I admired her so much. I told myself that one day, I'd have a big family, too. That I'd create the kind of love and chaos that felt like home.

But after having my fifth child, I knew, I couldn't do it again. Not because I didn't love my babies. But because I was tired. My body was tired. My spirit was tired. My dreams were still burning, but the weight of five little lives depending on me. It was a lot.

Even before I got pregnant with my youngest, I had thought about getting my tubes tied. I had wrestled with it quietly, in those moments of stillness when the house was finally quiet. I knew I wanted to focus on my career, build a better life, and breathe again.

When my baby girl was just four months old, I got the letter—I had been accepted into the Associate Degree in Nursing program. I remember holding her in one arm and reading the acceptance with the other, my eyes filling with tears. I had done it. Another step toward becoming a Registered Nurse. Another promise I could finally start keeping to myself. But the moment that joy hit, so did reality.

I was working sixteen-hour shifts on both Saturdays and Sundays— leaving before the sun came up and sometimes not walking back through the door until close to midnight. Monday through Friday, I was in class. I'd get the kids off to school, pull my hair back, grab my books, and head straight to campus. On the outside, I looked like I was making it work. But inside, I was barely hanging on.

And that's when the old cycle from Atlanta began to creep back in. He still wasn't working consistently. Some days he did small jobs. Most days, nothing. The weight of the household was back on my shoulders.

I told myself it was okay because he was at least home with the kids while I worked and went to school. That became my justification. *I can't leave— who else is going to watch the kids?* I said it like a fact, but it was really *a fear*. I didn't want to admit that I felt stuck again. But I wasn't thinking about leaving. I was thinking about finishing. Getting that degree. Passing my boards. Creating something better.

Even with all the hours I worked, it still wasn't enough. The bills kept piling up. Rent. Groceries. Tuition. Gas. Some nights, I laid in bed staring at the ceiling, wondering how I was going to stretch $100 into a week's worth of groceries and fuel.

That's when I thought about the home my father had purchased years ago. My grandmother had once lived there, but now the house sat empty. Our place in Elizabeth City had been big enough for all of us, but moving into my father's home meant lower rent—and I thought that would help us stay afloat while I finished school. So, I asked if we could move in. He said yes, but I'd still have to pay rent. I didn't argue. I was used to carrying the load.

We packed up and moved in, and for a while, it worked. The kids had a yard to play in. There was space to breathe. But when it came to school, I studied wherever I could—on the couch, in the car, at the kitchen table late at night while everyone else slept. There were times I couldn't focus at home at all, so I'd scrape together enough money to check into a hotel for a night just so I could study without interruption and pass my exams.

And sometimes—when my mind was too tired to hold any more information—I'd slide my notes or flashcards under my pillow and sleep on them, almost like I hoped the knowledge would soak into me overnight. It wasn't perfect. But it felt like progress. And at that point, progress was enough to keep going.

When the Dream Almost Broke Me

I was just three or four months away from finally completing my Associate Degree in Nursing. I had come so far—years of sacrifice, long hours, sleepless nights, and studying wherever I could just to hold everything together. But now, my grades were starting to slip.

Something had to give. I had to make a choice—keep working long shifts to stay afloat or scale back and pour everything I had into finishing school. I chose school.

And that meant the bills went unpaid. I thought I could juggle things, even if barely. Rent was one of the first things I eased up on—thinking, this was my daddy's house... he knew I was trying. I figured I could just send whatever I had when I had it, and he'd understand.

Then one day, the phone rang. It was my father calling from Connecticut. His voice was calm, but firm. "Jackie," he said. "I'm having your uncle take you to court for failure to pay rent on the house."

I went quiet. I hadn't expected that—not from him. I had been hoping he'd understand. I was trying to stay afloat. I was almost at the finish line.

Then he continued, and his words cut deeper than the court notice itself. "I've been watching you. I see how hard you're working. But I also see that your husband isn't doing anything. Not even trying. Not even willing to get a job at Piggly Wiggly down the street."

He wasn't being cruel. He was being honest. And that honesty hit like a punch to the gut.

He couldn't be at the court hearing himself—he was still living in Connecticut—so he had my uncle handle everything. When I sat in that courtroom days later, heart pounding and pride crumbling, all I could think about was what my daddy had said.

He didn't do it to punish me. He did it to teach me a lesson. And the lesson was loud and clear: I was the only one fighting for this family. I was the one working 16-hour weekends. The one staying up late with textbooks. The one losing sleep, time, and peace—just trying to build something better.

And even still, I chose him. Not the father who tried to hold me accountable. Not myself. Not even my children, in that moment. I chose the man I kept believing could one day become what I needed—what we needed.

The judge gave us ten days to move. Ten days to pack up five children and try—again—to figure it out. We found another small two-bedroom trailer. It wasn't home. It was another stop in the cycle. There were seven of us once again, squeezed into tight spaces—myself, him, and our five children—filling up every corner of that trailer with noise, movement, and survival.

The kids slept wherever we could make it work—on couches, in crowded beds, sometimes curled up beside us, and other nights on pallets we made from blankets and folded sheets. I'd tiptoe around them at night, careful not to wake anyone, just trying to catch my breath in the quiet.

And one night, after everyone was finally asleep, I sat on the edge of the bed and looked around. Toys tucked in corners. Laundry spilling out of baskets. Soft breathing in the background. And in that stillness, I had a moment of painful clarity:

I was right back where I started. Still chasing stability. Still carrying the load alone. Still choosing him, even when it meant losing myself. Still hoping that love was enough to build something whole.

But deep down, I knew. Love wasn't enough. And I couldn't keep pretending I didn't already know that.

Section 5
The Emotional Toll of Holding On

By the time another decade passed, I wasn't holding on out of love anymore. I wasn't even holding on out of hope. I was just... *there*. Existing in the same house. Moving through the same routine. Waking up, making breakfast, going to work, checking homework, folding clothes. No spark. No dream. No expectation of change.

I had spent the first 10 to 15 years of our relationship believing that things would get better. That if I held on a little longer, if I just prayed a little harder, if I could be stronger, more patient, more loving, that somehow, he'd finally become the man I believed he could be. But after another 9 or 10 years of repeating the same cycle, that belief had disappeared.

I wasn't expecting apologies anymore. I wasn't holding my breath for changed behavior. There were no more *maybe this time* moments left inside me. I had accepted that this was my life. And instead of feeling anger or grief about it, I felt something worse. I felt... nothing.

Numbness had settled in like a fog. Quiet, thick, and heavy. I didn't cry anymore—not over him, not over us. I didn't even flinch at disappointments. I just brushed them off, kept moving. There were no more late-night arguments. No more pleading for him to try. No more hope that things could still be salvaged. I wasn't in survival mode—I was in shutdown mode.

I had learned to tune everything out. The broken promises. The silent treatment. The late nights. The empty words. I buried every bit of frustration so deep that it felt like part of my body. It lived in my shoulders, in the knot in my stomach, in the permanent tightness behind my eyes.

I remember staring at the wall one evening while folding a load of laundry and realizing I had no idea what day it was. I couldn't even remember what I had cooked for dinner the night before. I was just going through the motions.

I didn't dream anymore. I didn't journal. I didn't plan vacations. There was no space for me in that life—not mentally, not emotionally, not spiritually. The only thing I had room for was them. My children.

They were the reason I kept going. The reason I got up each day. The reason I didn't completely fall apart. I poured every ounce of what I had left into them. Into making sure they were okay. That they had clean clothes, warm food, help with homework, someone in the stands at their school events—even when I was bone tired.

At that point, I wasn't living for love. I was living for responsibility. For provision. For consistency. For them. And that became my identity. Not wife. Not woman. Just mother—on autopilot.

Shifting Focus – Staying Became a Means to an End

At some point, my reason for staying completely changed. I wasn't staying because I believed in a loving marriage anymore. I wasn't clinging to the dream of a two-parent household. I wasn't even staying out of fear. I was staying because, in a strange way... it made things easier.

I had already stepped fully into the role of provider. I was the one clocking in. The one paying the bills. The one signing the field trip forms, replacing outgrown shoes, making sure the lights stayed on, and the pantry stayed stocked. It might have sounded like all the more reason to leave. But in my mind, it became a reason to stay.

Because if I was going to work long hours, at least he was home with the kids. At least I knew they weren't being left alone. He could cook a meal, turn on cartoons, and lay out clothes. I told myself: They're safe. That's what matters. I didn't think about what they were absorbing.

My focus had narrowed so much that all I saw was the next shift, the next bill, the next thing I had to do to make sure they were okay.

Somewhere along the way, my husband stopped being a partner. He wasn't my teammate. He wasn't my support system. He wasn't even someone I could confide in. He was just... there.

Another body in the house. Another adult who, at the very least, could make sure no one opened the door for strangers or burned the house down while I was gone. There was no trust. No connection.

And in some twisted way, his presence became convenient. He wasn't contributing much. But if I had to choose between coming home to kids alone—or coming home to someone who could say "they ate already" or "they're in bed"—I chose the easier path.

Because I was tired. Because I was used to doing it all anyway. Because I had already made so many sacrifices to keep our family afloat... What was one more? And at that point, I had stopped asking what I deserved. Stopped dreaming about what love should look like. I wasn't trying to be happy anymore. I was just trying to function.

And staying, for now, was how I functioned.

A Bigger Purpose – The Sacrifices I Made for My Children

It wasn't just about keeping food on the table anymore—It was about building something better.

By this time, we had moved to Raleigh, North Carolina. I had made the decision to relocate for my oldest daughter, who was starting college. The plan was to co-grandparent with Meman's grandmother and father while she pursued her degree. I wanted her to know she had a village behind her. I wanted to do everything I could to support her next chapter—even if mine was still filled with sacrifice.

At the time, I had no idea that shortly after the move, I'd get news that would change everything. My mother's cancer had returned—for the second time. That phone call sent a shockwave through my entire body. I didn't have time to fall apart. I had to figure it out—fast. I needed to be there for my mom. I needed to show up for my daughter. And I still had four other children plus a grandchild at home who needed me more than ever.

So, I did what I always did—I pushed harder. I took on two jobs to make it work. On weekends, I worked three 12-hour night shifts at a behavioral health facility—Friday, Saturday, and Sunday from 8 PM to 8 AM. When my shift ended Monday morning, I'd get in the car, still in my scrubs, and drive two and a half hours to the town where my mother lived. I worked there at a home care agency throughout the week so I could help my sister take care of her. Then on Thursday night, I'd pack up, get back in the car, and drive all the way back to Raleigh to be with my children—just in time to start it all over again.

I lived like that for nine months. Nine months of barely seeing my children awake. Nine months of missing moments I would never get back. Nine months of snatching sleep wherever I could—sometimes in my car, sometimes on a couch, sometimes not at all.

I told myself, "This is for them. This is how I give my children the life I never had. This is how I create something permanent, place they could call home." I wasn't working just to survive anymore. I was working to *build*. I wanted to buy a house. I wanted roots. I wanted something that belonged to us—something no one could take away.

And I believed with my whole heart that it was worth it. But in the middle of it all, I never stopped to ask whether he was worth it. I didn't ask if he was showing up in the same way. I didn't ask what he was sacrificing. Because I was so focused on the finish line, I didn't realize I was dragging him across it. He wasn't pushing with me. He wasn't building with me. He was just there.

And I told myself that was enough. Because they—my children—were more than enough. And for me, that was reason enough to keep going.

Redefining Strength - No Longer Feeling Trapped

For the first time, I started to see myself as strong—and independent. Not because I had finally left. Not because I had broken free from the relationship. But because I had figured out how to survive inside it.

I didn't feel trapped anymore—because I had stopped focusing on him. I had stopped hoping. Stopped waiting. Stopped expecting anything from him other than to simply be present in the house. I had redirected all of my energy toward something bigger—my children—and the vision I had for their future.

I had a goal. A house. Stability. A life they didn't have to recover from. And I was willing to sacrifice whatever I had to in order to make that happen. I worked through exhaustion. I swallowed disappointment like it was part of breakfast. I quieted my own wants and needs so completely that I honestly couldn't even tell you what I liked or dreamed of during that time.

I was still putting my own happiness on hold—but I had convinced myself it didn't matter anymore. Because if my children were smiling, I was doing something right. If they had a warm bed, if they were laughing at dinner, if they came home to lights on and food in the fridge—I called that success. I told myself over and over again: If they're okay, I'm okay. But looking back now, I realize I was running on empty.

I had been so determined to keep everything going that I never stopped to check on myself. I didn't notice how numb I had become. How disconnected I was. How invisible I had started to feel, even in my own life.

I had spent years—years—fighting for something, only to realize *I* was the only one actually fighting. *I* was the one showing up. The one carrying the emotional weight. The one holding all the loose ends of a family that wasn't built on balance.

And my children? They were starting to feel the cracks, too. They didn't always say it, but I could see it in their eyes. In the way my older ones got quiet when things got tense. In the way my younger ones clung to me when I came home from work. In the way they started picking up on my exhaustion, mirroring my silence.

I told myself I was protecting them—but the truth was, they were watching everything. They were learning how to sacrifice their own needs. They were learning how to stretch themselves too thin. They were learning that love meant survival—not joy.

And even though I had stopped feeling trapped, I hadn't really been freed. I had just learned how to live inside the cage—by convincing myself that the lock didn't matter.

The Kids Were Watching—And It Was Changing Them

I had always told myself that as long as my kids were safe and loved, they would be okay. That if I worked hard enough, smiled big enough, kept them fed and clothed and hugged tightly at night, it would somehow shield them from the dysfunction they were growing up around. I told myself they wouldn't remember the chaos, the arguing, the tension in the air. I thought if I carried the weight silently, they'd stay untouched.

But over time, I started to notice the shifts. Subtle at first. Quiet. But real. My oldest daughter had already become a mother of two—and she was pregnant with her third. I could see the pressure in her eyes, the determination in the way she held her children. She wanted so badly to give them more, but part of her had learned to survive the way she saw me survive—through silent strength, through sacrifice. She was doing what I had done: giving her all while carrying more than she should have ever had to.

My son, once my talker, became quiet. He used to tell me stories, ask questions, sit next to me while I cooked and just talk. But as the years went on, he turned inward. He barely spoke about his feelings. He kept things to himself. Sports became his only outlet—the one place he could let out everything he couldn't say. I remember watching him on the field one day, pushing his body with a kind of silent desperation, and thinking, *Please don't become your father. Please break the cycle.*

My third child withdrew from everything. She would come home from school, drop her bag, and go straight to sleep. Not out of laziness—but escape. Rest was her retreat. In high school, she got two jobs and became the one who cooked dinner for her younger siblings on the nights I worked 16-hour shifts—from 7 in the morning to 11:30 at night. She took care of the house like it was hers. She carried my burdens without ever saying she was tired. And I never wanted that for her.

My fourth daughter was a daddy's girl. Her bond with him was different from the rest. She clung to him with a fierceness that reminded me of how I once held on—desperately trying to make something feel whole. She found safety in him, even when he wasn't always consistent. Her loyalty to him was strong—like she was guarding a version of him she hoped was real.

And my youngest baby became my shadow. She was always by my side, watching me, needing me closer. She wouldn't go to sleep unless I was in the room. She'd follow me from one part of the house to another, silently tracking me as if being too far away might make her disappear. And I let her cling to me, even when I was too tired to carry anything else. Because part of me needed her, too.

None of them ever asked why I was gone so much. But I know they noticed. I know they wondered why Mama always looked tired. Why I was quiet at the dinner table. Why my hugs lingered just a little longer, like I was apologizing without words. And deep down, I think they understood.

They knew this was how I kept everything together. They saw me doing what needed to be done. And **that** was the problem. Because holding everything together was slowly breaking me apart. And they were learning how to do the same.

All The Signs I Didn't Want To See

There were so many moments I should have left. I should have left when I saw my oldest daughter crying over a boy who disrespected her—watching her live out a version of the relationship she had grown up seeing. I saw the way she tried to shrink her emotions, how she made excuses for his behavior, how she fought for someone who wasn't showing up for her—and it broke me. Because I knew exactly where she learned it.

I should have left when I realized I was working 64-hour weeks just to keep us afloat. Waking up before sunrise, putting on scrubs, driving through exhaustion. The bills were stacking—mortgage, lights, groceries, insurance, car notes—over $4,000 a month. And somehow, I was the only one doing the math, the only one losing sleep over how to stretch a dollar.

I should have left when he told me he was going to work, and I'd watch him walk out the door with empty hands—and come back the same way. No paycheck. No explanation. No effort to contribute. Just more silence, more excuses, more weight added to my shoulders while I kept pretending it was normal.

I should have left every time my body gave me warning signs—when my chest tightened from stress, when my back ached from double shifts, when I cried in the car but wiped my face before walking in the house so the kids wouldn't see. I should have left when I felt my own joy disappearing when the silence between us became louder than the arguments ever were.

I should have left so many times, but I didn't. I stayed. Because I told myself I had made it this far. Because I told myself my kids needed me to keep everything stable. Because I didn't want to admit that the family I had fought so hard to hold together had already fallen apart.

And by the time I realized it, the cost of holding on too long was already showing. It was showing in my tired eyes. In my children's quiet sadness. In the weight of the dreams, I'd buried just to survive another day.

Section 6
The First Sign of a Generational Cycle:
Watching History Repeat Itself

I always told myself, my children would have better than what I had. Better than what I endured. Better than the cycles I had grown up trapped in. I thought that by keeping our family together, I was giving them something solid. That the sacrifices I made—the sleepless nights, the financial juggling, the emotional silencing—were all for their good. I believed that by enduring what I had endured, I was shielding them. That somehow, my pain would serve as a covering. But life has a way of showing us the truth—slowly at first, then all at once.

The first crack came when I watched my oldest daughter in a relationship that mirrored mine far too closely. I saw the hesitation in her voice when she spoke about him. The way she downplayed the disrespect. The way she tried to "keep the peace" even when her peace was being stolen from her.

She was holding on too long. Fighting for someone who wasn't fighting for her. And it felt like I was watching my younger self through her eyes.

And then there was my son. My only boy. The one I had tried so hard to raise differently. The one I had prayed over. Covered. Watched closely.

Loved deeply. But slowly, I started to see him pulling away. Not just from me—but from himself.

He started mimicking the same behaviors I had once begged his father to change. The cold silence. The emotional distance. The need to be in control of every situation. The refusal to open up, even when it was clear he was hurting. I realized that he had learned not through my words—but through my patterns. All the times I had told him, "Don't be like that. Don't treat a woman like that. Don't shut down."

They were drowned out by the example he had lived through. And suddenly, all those years of me staying didn't look like protection anymore. They looked like *permission*. And it was devastating. Because I didn't just see my mistakes—I saw my legacy.

I saw the cost of holding on too long ripple through the very lives I was trying to save. For the first time, I had to admit: my children had learned from me. Not from what I preached, but from what I lived. They had learned how to survive. How to sacrifice. How to stay. And I couldn't undo what they had seen.

My Daughter – The Same Cycle, The Same Struggles

The first red flag should've been when she got pregnant at 15 and gave birth on her 16th birthday. I remember sitting beside her in the hospital, holding her hand as the contractions came, the same way I had once gritted through that pain when I was around her age.

And it hit me—I had done everything I could to prevent this. I tried to open her eyes early. When she was younger, I even had her in the delivery room with me during her sister's birth. I thought that if she saw the reality— the blood, the pain, the rawness of childbirth—it would be enough to steer her away from it.

But three years later, there she was. Sixteen. A mother. Just like I had been. And I never could've imagined then that fourteen years later, the child she brought into the world that day—my Meman—would be gone. Gone because of suicide. Gone before the cycle ever had a chance to truly be broken.

At the time, I told myself this was just a misstep. She was young. She still had time to recover, to regroup, to rewrite her story. I wasn't going to abandon her—I was going to do for her what no one had done for me.

I said, "Go to school. Focus on your education. I'll help with the baby while you build a future for yourself." And for a little while, she did.

She enrolled in a university. She studied. She had plans. And I was right there beside her, holding the pieces together. But then, four years later, she had another child.

And something in me shifted.

I had reached my limit—not in love, but in the sacrifices I knew I couldn't keep making. I looked at her and said, "I can help with one. But I will not raise two. This is your life now. You have to take responsibility for your choices." She dropped out of college and became a full-time mom.

And just a few years after that, she had a third child—this time with a man who was nothing more than an opportunist. A man who reminded me too much of her father.

I watched her juggle it all. Work long hours. Pay every bill. Hustle to keep food on the table. Struggle to maintain housing. She carried the full weight of her home—while the man who called himself *her partner* sat back and benefited from her every effort.

And it was like watching my own life play out all over again. She didn't have to say a word—I could see it in her eyes. The tiredness. The pressure. The sadness she tried to cover up with a half-smile. The same way I once did.

Then one day, she called me in a panic. Her voice was shaking. She had gone outside to take the kids to school and her car was gone. They had repossessed it. She had fallen behind on the payments—again.

And even though I was tired, even though I was juggling my own responsibilities, I didn't hesitate. I got her car back. I paid what needed to be paid. I made sure she had what she needed to keep going for her kids.

And that wasn't the only time it happened. It became a pattern. And what made it worse was knowing that the boyfriend—the one who contributed nothing—had been the one driving the car the whole time. He didn't even have a license. And the only thing he ever contributed to was tearing it up.

She worked. She sacrificed. And he reaped the benefits while offering nothing in return. At that moment, I felt so many things—helpless, frustrated, and deeply, deeply heartbroken. I had spent my whole life trying to pave a better road for her. Trying to give her the wisdom I had earned the hard way. But here she was—walking the same path, step for step.

I tried to talk to her. I tried to pour every ounce of my experience into my words. I told her, "I've lived this life. I know how this ends. You don't have to prove anything. You deserve better."

But deep down I knew the truth. How could I expect her to listen to what I said when I had spent most of her childhood showing her something else?

My Son – The Weight of an Unseen Influence

My son was always different from my daughters. He was quiet, observant, and kept everything locked inside. While my girls expressed their emotions—sometimes loudly—he chose silence. He didn't ask for much and rarely shared what he was going through. But on the field? That's where he came alive.

Sports were his therapy. His release. His language. When he played, I saw glimpses of the fire inside him. The passion. The potential. And every time he stepped onto that field, I whispered a silent prayer: Let this be the thing that saves him.

I was always intentional with my words. I'd tell him, "You don't have to be like your father. You are better than that. You can be more than that."

But the truth was—he didn't have any other example of what a man was supposed to be. His father was there, physically. He lived in the house. But emotionally, mentally, and financially, he was absent, at least for me anyway. There was no consistency. No affection. No guidance. No follow-through. Just presence without purpose. Silence where there when there should have been leadership.

And even though I tried to model everything I could, there were things I just couldn't teach him as a mother.

When my son graduated high school, I hoped he'd go to college—he had the talent, the discipline, the drive. But he chose technical school instead. He said he wanted to be a mechanic. I supported his choice without hesitation. I was proud of him for having a plan, for wanting to work with his hands and build something of his own.

But just a few months in, I got a phone call I'd never forget. It was from his school—his housing advisor. They said, "We found marijuana in the dorm. Your son's roommate missed so many days of class, so we went to do a wellness check. That's when we discovered the smell and found the drugs." Even though the weed wasn't his, they were holding both boys accountable.

Then came the blow: "You have 24 hours to come get him, or his belongings will be put on the curb." I dropped everything. I got in the car, my heart pounding the entire way. I remember the ache in my chest—anger, worry, sadness, confusion all swirling at once. I wanted to believe it was just a misunderstanding. I wanted to believe this wouldn't be the end of his journey.

But it was. He was expelled. Just like that, his dream of becoming a mechanic, snatched out from under him.

After that, he started working construction. At first, I thought it was temporary. Just something to get by. But then he started traveling out of state—to work with his dad. And my heart sank.

Then came the part that hurt the most—just like his father, he never brought money home. I tried to talk to him. Asked him gently, then firmly. "What are you doing with your money? Why aren't you helping out?" He had no answers. Or maybe, he just didn't know how to say them out loud.

Not long after that, he met a girl in South Carolina. And before I could wrap my head around it, he married her. I didn't know about the wedding. I didn't get an invitation. I didn't even get a phone call until after the vows were already said.

To make it worse, that same night, I was in the hospital with my grandmother—watching her take her final breaths. I was saying goodbye to one life while missing one of the biggest milestones in another.

And once again, I felt history creeping back in—repeating itself, step by painful step.

That marriage didn't bring him peace. It brought chaos. Stress. Legal trouble. Emotional confusion. At one point, he ended up with a criminal record—not for something he had done, but for taking the blame for someone else. When I finally asked him, "Why would you do that? Why would you risk everything for someone who wouldn't do the same for you?"

His response left me speechless.

"I never really saw any other relationships or marriages other than yours and Dad's. I thought that was how love was supposed to be." And in that moment, I felt the floor beneath me crack. I had told him for years—be better than me. I had poured into him, warned him, prayed over him.

But my words didn't matter. What mattered was what he saw. And what he saw—day after day, year after year—was a woman who stayed. Who worked. Who carried it all. And that became his definition of love. Not what I said. But what I lived.

The Mirror My Children Held Up to Me

For years, I told myself I was staying for my kids. That keeping our family together would protect them from the pain I had known growing up. That my sacrifices would give them stability, security, and a childhood free from the fear of being left behind.

I believed I was doing the right thing. I believed love meant staying. I believed suffering in silence was a noble kind of strength. But somewhere along the way, that belief started to unravel.

The more I watched my oldest children repeat my story—the toxic relationships, the emotional shutdowns, the financial struggle—the more I realized: I hadn't been protecting them at all. They weren't learning from what I said. They were learning from what I lived.

I could hear my oldest daughter justifying her boyfriend's behavior the way I once had—making excuses, hoping love could change him.

I could see my son holding back his emotions, trying to be the "man" he thought his father was—quiet, distant, emotionally unavailable.

And I noticed my third daughter—the one who rarely asked for help—always making her way back home when she wasn't working. She'd quietly slip through the door, drop her bag, and go lie across her bed without saying much, or either go cook a meal when there were barely any food in the home. She didn't need to speak—I could feel the exhaustion in her body, the pressure she carried without ever calling it by name.

I saw the weight in all of their eyes. The patterns forming. The hope fading.

And one evening, while folding laundry in the quiet of our home, my younger daughters ran into the room. They were laughing, light and full of energy, completely unaware of the heaviness that lingered in the air. They danced around me, giggling, asking what was for dinner.

And as I looked up at them, a lump rose in my throat. *It's not too late for them*, I thought. *But it will be if I don't do something now.* I knew I couldn't go back and rewrite the past. I couldn't undo what my older children had seen. I couldn't unteach what they had learned from watching me survive rather than thrive.

But I could draw a line. I could choose differently. I could show my younger children what healing looked like in real time—not in theory, not in books, but in action. I could finally choose myself—not because I stopped loving them, but because I wanted to love them better.

I just didn't know if I had the strength to do it yet. Because choosing different meant owning the damage I had normalized. It meant confronting the life I had built from brokenness. It meant stepping out of the role I had mastered—the woman who held it all together at any cost.

But deep in my spirit, something was shifting. A quiet voice began to rise. *You've done hard things before. You can do this, too. You just have to choose **you**.*

The Last Lesson Staying had to Teach

Looking back, I see now that staying wasn't just about love or fear—it was about the version of strength I had been taught. I thought *endurance* made me noble. I thought *silence* made me safe. But the truth is, strength isn't about how much you can carry—it's about knowing when to let go. It's about seeing the impact of your choices on the people you love and having the courage to choose a new path, even when your knees are shaking. I didn't have all the answers. But I had a deep understanding: it was time to stop surviving the life I had and start building the life I needed.

CHAPTER 3

The Moment I knew
I Had To Leave for Good

It wasn't one single moment that broke me. It was a slow piling on—year after year, disappointment after disappointment. A series of heavy, invisible bricks stacked on my back until my knees quietly buckled beneath me.

And still, I kept going.

For years, I convinced myself I was holding my family together. I clung to that belief like it was a badge of honor. But the truth was, I wasn't holding anything together. I was the only one carrying it. And the weight was crushing me.

Every month, I paid over $4,000 just to keep us afloat—mortgage, utilities, phone bills, insurance, car payments. That didn't include groceries, school supplies, gas, clothing, or anything extra the kids needed. I was working 64 hours a week, trying to maintain a life that looked "stable" on the outside, even though it was slowly collapsing behind closed doors.

I didn't want my children to just survive. I wanted them to live.

I wanted them to have what I never had—memories that weren't rooted in survival. I wanted them to be able to go to school events, play sports, go to the movies with friends, and wear clothes that fit right. I didn't want them to feel like every day was about scraping by or waiting for the next crisis.

And the man who was supposed to be my partner? He was working, too, but somehow, he never had anything to show for it. No money for the light bill. No money for groceries. No help with gas. Just empty explanations and a quiet expectation that I'd figure it out.

It made me sick to my stomach.

Every time a bill came, every time the kids needed something, every time I filled up the gas tank with my last twenty dollars—I felt that resentment creeping in. And on the days I wasn't working, the tension was even worse.

Because on those days, I had to hide the car keys.

This was the same car I had helped my daughter get back—the one that had been repossessed multiple times. The same car I had sacrificed for. And now I had to hide the keys like a parent hiding candy from a child, because I refused to let him keep driving it like it was his.

He wasn't helping. He wasn't contributing. But he still felt entitled to the little bit of peace I had scraped together.

I said, "You can use it when I'm working. That's it. Take our daughter to the bus stop, and then park it. That's the deal." He continued to use the car for so-called work, that he still never brought home any money nor had money to replenish the gas for the car.

But when I was off? The keys stayed hidden in my purse, in my dresser drawer, or tucked away somewhere he wouldn't find them. Because I wasn't about to let him wreck or lose the one thing I had worked so hard to restore.

That's the kind of reality I was living in. Not trust. Not teamwork. Just survival strategy.

And still—I got up. Still—I made sure the kids were good. Still—I went to work. Still—I told myself, just a little longer. But inside, I was unraveling.

I had mastered the art of pretending everything was fine. I smiled when I was supposed to. I nodded during conversations. I laughed when people asked how I was doing. But inside, I was running on fumes—physically exhausted, emotionally numb, spiritually drained.

And I started to wonder: How long can I do this? How much more of myself do I have left to give? Because I was holding everything together. But nothing was holding me.

When the Silence Said Everything

He had a stable job. A full-time position as a maintenance supervisor at an assisted living facility—not even five minutes from our home. He clocked in every day, wore his uniform, answered to a boss. On paper, he was employed. Responsible. A man with income.

But somehow that income never made it home. Not to the bills. Not to the kids. Not to me.

Every month, I looked at our finances—and it was my name on everything. My paycheck covered the mortgage, the light bill, the food, and the gas. My hands kept everything running.

And him? Empty pockets. Shrugged shoulders. Silence.

I was working nonstop—busting my ass to make sure the lights stayed on, that the kids had clean clothes, that the fridge wasn't empty. I was clocking 64 hours a week, running this house like a full-time operation. Meanwhile, he moved through it like a visitor.

Then one afternoon, I came home from a long shift and found him sitting at the kitchen table—comfortable, relaxed, like life was good. The TV was on. He was eating. Wearing the clothes I had washed. Sitting in the home that I was breaking my back to hold together.

And I just stared at him.

He didn't even notice at first. Didn't ask how my day was. Didn't offer to help with dinner. He sat there like a man *entitled* to peace that he didn't earn.

And in that stillness, something cracked open in me. How did I get here? How did I let a grown man sit in my house, eat the food I bought, sleep in the bed I paid for, and contribute absolutely nothing?

I didn't yell. I didn't throw anything. I didn't even speak. But inside me, everything got louder. The part of me that used to defend him—the one that used to say, "He's trying," or "It's just a rough patch"—was growing quiet.

And the other part? The part of me that was exhausted? That was angry? That was tired of building a life with someone who was just along for the ride?

That voice? It was rising louder than my fear. Louder than my guilt. Louder than the excuses I had whispered to myself for far too long.

That night, I couldn't sleep.

I lay in the dark, listening to the hum of the ceiling fan and the soft, steady breathing of a man who had no idea that I was drifting further away with every passing day.

I wasn't angry anymore. I was **numb**. I stared at the ceiling and let the truth settle into my bones: This wasn't a marriage. It hadn't been for a long time. *I* had been carrying it. Fighting for it. Funding it. Covering it up and holding it down. But the silence that night said everything. And I finally stopped pretending that it was love.

The First Step Toward Letting Go

I had spent twenty-three years being loyal. Loyal to a man who had lied to me. Cheated on me. Drained me—financially, emotionally, spiritually. Physically and emotionally abused me. For over two decades, I had defended him to others. Explained away his behavior. Justified his absence. Carried the weight of our family on my back while he disappeared into excuses. I gave my all to a man who never learned how to give anything back.

And then one day, something unexpected happened.

I was working my shift as the HUB nurse on the Child and Adolescent Unit (CAU) at a psychiatric hospital. My job as a HUB nurse was to serve as the bridge between leadership and frontline staff. I had just responded to an intervention with the team, and after things settled, I was reviewing documentation at the nurses' station. My mind was still focused on clinical notes, the seclusion and restraints documentation, and de-escalation write-ups when one of my coworkers passed by and quietly slipped a folded piece of paper into my hand.

His number. I paused.

In twenty-three years of marriage, I had never accepted anything like that. Not a compliment. Not a look. Not a conversation that felt too familiar. I had been faithful—loyal to a fault. I didn't entertain what-ifs or maybes. I never allowed space for anything that looked like temptation. But this time, I didn't give it back. I didn't crumple it up or toss it out.

I tucked it into the side pocket of my scrub pockets beneath my lip gloss and the notes I had scribbled on the back of a med sheet. Not because I wanted a relationship. Not because I was searching for attention. And not even because I was interested in him. It was about what that moment revealed about me.

Because for the first time in my marriage, I didn't feel obligated to protect what no longer felt sacred. I didn't feel guilty. I didn't feel fear. I didn't feel married in the ways that mattered most.

Instead, I felt clarity. A quiet awareness that had been growing in me for years finally spoke loud enough to be heard: You've already emotionally left this marriage. This is just the first time you're admitting it. This was *real*. It was about acknowledging that I had stopped choosing a man who had long stopped choosing me. And that realization—spoken not in confrontation, but in the softness of one small decision—was the beginning of the end.

Because once you start reaching for something more, you stop pretending you're okay with having less.

The Guilt, The Realization, and The Final Goodbye

Later that night, I was driving home from work—physically exhausted, but emotionally even more worn down.

I had just finished a long shift and was replaying everything in my mind: the phone number still tucked in my scrub pocket, the long years I had poured into a one-sided marriage, and the weight of what it meant to even consider letting go.

That's when my phone rang. It was one of my kids. "Mom, can you stop and bring us something to eat?" I said *yes*, but I was barely paying attention to the road. My thoughts were heavy, fogging up everything else.

And that's when it happened. I didn't realize how fast I was going until I saw the flashing blue lights in my rear-view mirror. Pulled over. Ticketed. Clocked doing way over the speed limit.

As I sat there on the side of the road, holding that piece of paper, it felt like more than a speeding ticket. It felt like a message. Like a consequence. Like maybe I was being punished—not just for speeding, but for where my heart and mind had been drifting lately.

Maybe this is karma, I told myself. *Maybe I was wrong for accepting that number. Maybe I should just keep trying, just keep holding on.*

But a few days later, that guilt started to dissolve. I was sitting alone in my room, staring at the same crumpled piece of paper that I had put in my scrub pocket, and I thought, *You already got the ticket. Might as well make it worth it.*

So, I called him. And I met up with him. It wasn't casual. It wasn't innocent. It was intimate. And it was the first time in twenty-three years that another man touched me besides my ex-husband. And in that moment, I knew—this wasn't just emotional detachment anymore.

This was final. This was the end. I didn't cry. I didn't feel shame. What I felt was clarity. Because I had already left emotionally. I had already left mentally. And that night—I left physically.

It took me another two years to leave the marriage in the legal sense. Two more years of trying. Of hoping. Of watching the same patterns replay themselves like clockwork. Two more years of carrying the entire weight of our household while he still couldn't—or wouldn't—pay a damn light bill.

But when I finally filed for divorce, it was different this time. I wasn't angry. I wasn't sad. I was **done**. I had already said goodbye long before the paperwork was signed. And this time, I meant it.

Section 2
Preparing to Leave

Taking Back Control

When I finally picked up the divorce packet from the courthouse, I didn't cry. I didn't tremble. I didn't second-guess myself. I walked out of there with something I hadn't felt in years—relief. The kind of relief that doesn't come with celebration but with a quiet exhale. A release. A deep, settling knowing that I was finally doing something for me.

Even though the packet felt thick and heavy in my hands—pages filled with legal language I had to read twice, sometimes three times—I held it like it was freedom. I took it home and sat at the kitchen table, flipping through every page slowly, methodically. Pen in hand. Hot chocolate growing cold beside me. I let the silence wrap around me like a blanket.

As I started filling out those forms, I felt like I was writing the final chapter of a story I had been stuck in for far too long. The end of a book I never wanted to finish but knew I had to. And as much as I felt peace, I also felt shame. Shame that it had taken stepping outside of my marriage to fully see how far gone it already was. Shame that I had compromised my own values just to feel something again—something human, something alive.

It hit me all at once—I should've been **done** a long time ago. I should've been done when I walked in and saw him in bed with another woman. I should've been done when he left the kids stranded at school with no ride home. I should've been done when he threw me across the car like I didn't matter. I should've been done when he headbutted me over a gold tooth I got at eighteen. A moment so senseless, so violent, that it left a scar I still carry to this day.

But I wasn't done. I stayed. And for years, I told myself it was for the kids. For the family. For love. But if I'm being honest—it was fear. Fear of the unknown. Fear of being alone. Fear of failure. Fear that I wouldn't be enough without him, even though he had never truly been there for me. I had been with him since I was sixteen. By the time I was forty-one, I had spent over half my life waiting for a man to change. And he never did.

Even when I started stepping outside the marriage—something I never imagined I would do—I still hoped he'd notice. I hoped the shift in me would spark something in him. That maybe he'd finally wake up. Fight for me. Choose me.

But he didn't. All he did was grow jealous. Ask questions. Get suspicious. But never once did he stop and say, "I see I'm losing you. Let me do better." Never once did he choose the hard work over the easy excuses. Never once did he try to rebuild what he spent years tearing down. So, as I signed each line on that divorce packet, I didn't feel like a failure. I felt like a woman reclaiming her power. Because this time, I wasn't waiting on him to change. I was choosing to change my life.

Still Sharing a Roof, Still Feeling Trapped

We were still living under the same roof when I filed for divorce. And let me tell you—that was one of the hardest parts. Because while I was working to free myself, I still felt like a prisoner inside my own home.

He knew the divorce was coming. This wasn't a surprise. I had given him a warning—two full years in advance. I told him flat out, "You've got two years to get it together. Two years to be the man you promised to be. Or I'm gone." And what did he do with those two years? Nothing. No effort. No change. No accountability. He didn't step up. Didn't start paying bills. Still couldn't cover something as simple as the light bill—even after twenty-five years.

So, I started packing. Boxing up his things. Quietly closing the door on a life I had fought to hold together. I folded his clothes. Packed up his shoes. Gathered his personal items and started placing them into boxes—calmly, piece by piece. But every time I packed something, he unpacked it. Took things right back out. Put them right back where they were. Like he could undo my decision by pretending it wasn't real.

Like if he didn't acknowledge it, maybe it wouldn't happen. The tension in that house was unbearable. We argued over everything and nothing. Some nights were full of silence. Other nights, the air felt so thick with unspoken resentment, I could barely breathe. I told him when the court date was. Told him what time to be there. Made sure he had no excuses.

According to my oldest daughter, he went down to the courthouse early that morning—before I ever arrived. He asked someone at the desk, "What happens if one party doesn't show up?" When they told him the divorce would still go through, he made sure not to come. But not because he was ready to let go. Not because he wanted it to happen. He didn't show up because he was scared. Scared of what I might say. Scared of hearing me speak the truth out loud in front of a judge. Scared that I might lay bare all the things I had carried silently for so long.

So, I sat in that courtroom by myself. Alone but not broken. And when the judge stamped those papers—when the divorce became official—I felt a wave of everything all at once: Grief. Peace. Anger. Relief. Freedom. And a strange, quiet joy. Because that moment wasn't just the end of a marriage. It was the beginning of me. I wasn't just walking away from him. I was walking back home to myself.

The Breaking Point – Leaving for Good

When I got home from the courthouse, divorce papers fresh in my hands, the man I had just legally separated from was sitting in my house like nothing had happened. Feet up. Remote in hand. Acting like everything was business as usual—like the weight of the day hadn't changed a thing. And something in me just snapped.

I looked at him and said, "You need to leave. It's done. This is no longer your home."

But instead of standing up and owning the reality, he exploded. He puffed out his chest and said, "I ain't going a G-damn place." Just like that. As if the twenty-five years of damage, the divorce papers, the judge's decision meant absolutely nothing. As if he could still bulldoze his way through the truth and intimidate me into staying silent. But not this time.

We went back and forth for hours. Voices rising. Tension thick enough to choke on. Every old wound between us surfaced in that moment—years of betrayal, disappointment, silence, rage—it all came pouring out like gasoline on fire. And in the middle of that storm, I realized just how unsafe I felt. Not just physically but emotionally. Spiritually. I was no longer arguing to be heard—I was arguing to protect my peace. So, I made the call.

I picked up the phone and called my daughter and her child's father in Texas. My voice shook but I didn't stutter. I said, "Y'all need to come get these kids. Because either their mama and daddy are going to jail, or somebody's going to end up dead."

I wasn't being dramatic. I was done.

He refused to leave. Still. Even after everything. He sat there like a squatter in the ruins of the life I had just walked away from. Still trying to control the air in the room. Still trying to act like he had a say.

I packed a bag and walked out of my own house that night.

I went to stay with a friend—someone I called my sister. Someone who had opened her door for me before and did it again without hesitation. I needed space to breathe. To think. To feel the full weight of what I had just done.

And even in the middle of all that chaos, I already had a plan for what came next.

I had planned a weekend beach trip for me and the kids. A celebration. A soft reset. Something light to remind them—and me—that just because things fell apart, didn't mean that joy couldn't still find its way in. We needed that trip. We needed that moment. We needed the reminder that freedom, even when it started messy, was still sacred. Because I wasn't just trying to rebuild life after divorce—I was trying to show my children what it looked like to start over without losing yourself.

My Daughter's Response

I had told my oldest daughter about the divorce beforehand. She wasn't shocked. Not really. She had seen the changes in me long before I ever said the words. She noticed how I was moving differently—how my laughter had a little more air in it, how I stopped walking around on eggshells, how I started doing small things just for me again. She never asked directly, but she knew I had a "special friend." She didn't need me to say it—she saw it in my energy. My peace. My posture. She saw a woman slowly coming back to life.

One day, I told her, "Be on the lookout. Some things are going to start coming in the mail for your dad." She paused for a second then let out this soft little laugh. Not the kind that mocked or judged. It was a knowing laugh. A sisterhood kind of laugh. Like she had been quietly rooting for me all along—waiting for the day I'd finally choose myself. There was no lecture. No disappointment in her voice. Just a quiet respect. And maybe even a little pride.

When I finally said it out loud—that the divorce was real, that it was done, that I was free—something in me exhaled. And she just nodded, like she already knew. And in that moment, I felt peace. Not the kind of peace that comes after a fight. Not the kind that feels temporary. But the kind that comes when you finally do what you were meant to do. The kind of peace that feels like home. Because my daughter wasn't just witnessing my healing—she was experiencing her own through it. And that made everything worth it.

Letting Go of 25 Years

I spent twenty-five years covering for this man. Twenty-five years minimizing, explaining, absorbing the blows—both literally and emotionally—so that nobody else saw the truth I was living with every day.

I protected him from judgment. I shielded him from consequences. I stayed quiet when I should've spoken up. I let people believe he was better than he was—because I thought that somehow made me better, too. That's how he had conditioned me. To believe that his peace mattered more than mine. That his reputation was more important than my truth.

That if I just tried harder, gave more, bent a little further, everything would eventually fall into place. So, I internalized it all. The disappointments. The betrayals. The bruises no one saw.

I wore the weight of his failures like they were mine. And every time someone asked how I was doing, I smiled. Nodded. Lied.

But after the divorce was finalized—after that judge stamped those papers and I walked out into the fresh air with my head high—I felt something inside of me finally shift. I stopped protecting him. Stopped carrying his guilt. Stopped sacrificing myself so he wouldn't have to feel uncomfortable.

And for the first time in years, I didn't second-guess it. There was no question in my heart. No wondering if I had made the right decision. No temptation to reach back. Because I had stayed too long. I had lost myself too many times. And I had paid the price—physically, emotionally, spiritually.

So no, I wasn't going back. Not for the kids. Not for the history. Not for the version of love I had spent two decades trying to make real. This time, I was done. For real. No more second chances. No more shrinking to keep someone else comfortable. No more settling for survival and calling it stability.

This wasn't just the end of a marriage. This was the beginning of the life I was finally choosing—on my terms. A life rooted in peace. In truth. In joy. A life where my children would see their mother whole, not hiding. Because I wasn't just letting go of a man. I was letting go of 25 years of silence, sacrifice, and self-abandonment. And in return, I was finally choosing me.

Section 3
Life After Letting Go

February 21, 2015. I thought that date would mark the beginning of my freedom. I had finally done it. After years of back-and-forth, betrayal, heartbreak, and disappointment, I was officially divorced. I expected to feel weightless. I expected to feel free. I thought I'd walk out of that courthouse with a sense of peace washing over me like a clean slate.

But that's not what happened. That very night, we got into one of the worst fights we'd ever had. The kind that shakes the walls and makes you question if freedom is even real when fear still lives in your house. Because despite the judge's signature, I still felt like a prisoner in my own home.

For months after the divorce, I had to live with the weight of him still lingering. I had to change the locks because he never returned the keys. Every time I stepped outside, I'd find myself looking over my shoulder. I couldn't shake the fear that he might be watching, waiting, showing up uninvited.

That fear didn't disappear just because I signed some papers. I had to live with it. Breathe through it. Parent through it.

Things came to a head during the kids' school track-out. I decided to take them to Texas to visit their older sister. And I took him with us—not out of love, not out of any hope of reconciliation—but because once again, he had nowhere to go. I thought maybe if I dropped him off to live with our adult daughter, it would be the final tie cut. That maybe, just maybe, we could finally be free of each other.

And just like always—he didn't help. Not with gas. Not with food. Not with anything we needed to make that trip happen. And when we got there, nothing changed. He didn't help her either. Wouldn't contribute to bills. Wouldn't step up. Wouldn't offer anything more than the bare minimum—just like always. That arrangement didn't last long.

When I returned to North Carolina, I came back alone. The girls stayed behind to enjoy their break with their sister. And I'd never forget how it felt driving home. There was a stillness inside me, one I hadn't known in years. I could breathe. He was finally several states away. I didn't have to rehearse what I'd say next. I didn't have to brace myself for another guilt trip or manipulation tactic. He was gone. And I was free.

About three months later I moved to Houston for a job opportunity. A fresh start. Being around my children and grandchild gave me purpose again. It gave me focus. It gave me joy. And just a month later, my oldest daughter made her own bold decision—she left her child's father and moved to Texas, too. Life was shifting again.

At one point, I asked him if he could send something to help with the girls. His answer? "No." And honestly, it stung—but it didn't surprise me. He hadn't helped when we were together. Why would he start now?

Even a year after the divorce, when we were still in Texas, I never let him know where we lived. That's how deeply the fear still lived inside me. He only took the girls school shopping once. Some supplies. A few outfits. Just enough to say he did something.

When we eventually moved back to North Carolina, he started calling again. Not to check on the girls. Not to see how they were doing. He called with requests. "Can you pick me up from the airport? I got a job lined up in North Carolina."

My response? "HELL no." He didn't get access to me anymore. He didn't get to show up and disrupt the peace I had fought so hard to build.

Then came the questions about the man I had been seeing—the one I had stepped out of my marriage with. And for the first time in all these years, I didn't feel guilty. I didn't shrink. I didn't stumble. I didn't explain. Because I had finally chosen me.

The girls were okay at first. They spoke to him occasionally. They saw him when we visited my older daughters in Fort Worth. But over time, the connection faded. He only called when it benefited him. One day, I asked my youngest how she felt about her dad. Her answer was simple, honest, and heavy: "I feel numb. It is what it is."

That's when it hit me. My girls were growing. They were adjusting. They were healing in ways I had prayed for. And we were okay. Just the three of us. I didn't need anyone else to make our house feel like a home. The fear was gone. The weight was gone. And for the first time in decades, I felt light.

My relationship was growing stronger. The girls were thriving. We were building something new—slowly, but beautifully. And I realized something that brought both clarity and pain: All those years I thought I was protecting them by staying, I was really teaching them that love meant pain. That stability came with sacrifice. That survival was the same thing as peace. But they had seen it all. And now, so had I.

And through it all—God never left me. Even in my silence. Even in my fear. Even in the moments I chose everyone else but myself. He never gave me more than I could bear. He carried me through the storm. And when I was ready—He showed me that everything I went through had purpose. This was my season of release. My season of rising. And I wasn't turning back.

Section 4
Breaking the Cycle for the Ones Still Watching

After the divorce, things didn't magically get better overnight. Healing wasn't instant—it was messy, layered, and deeply emotional. It took me nearly a year and a half, maybe even closer to two years, to truly feel peace. But once that peace settled in, I knew something inside me had shifted for good. For the first time in decades, I didn't feel like I had to look over my shoulder. I wasn't constantly bracing myself for chaos. I could exhale—and that breath was freedom.

And what a difference that made—not just for me, but for my girls.

My two youngest daughters were still at home, still watching, still absorbing everything. But this time, the version of me they saw was different. I was no longer surviving, I was living. I was softer, calmer, and more present. The storm had finally passed and now there was space for peace. That peace became the foundation I started parenting from.

With them, I was intentional. I didn't just want to give them structure— I wanted to give them safety. Emotional safety. A home where they could express themselves, where love wasn't loud and angry, where they didn't have to tiptoe or decode moods. They had room to grow without carrying the weight of dysfunction.

I wasn't pretending anymore. I wasn't covering bruises with smiles or masking exhaustion with fake strength. I had made it out, and I was determined to do it differently. I protected their innocence, their space, and their energy in a way I hadn't been able to for the older kids. And while that realization still brings a pang of guilt sometimes, I now understand that doing better when you know better is the healing.

There were small signs that the cycle was breaking. My youngest daughter once said, "It is what it is," when I asked about her relationship with her father. Not bitter. Not broken. Just aware. That moment told me everything. She wasn't clinging to pain. She wasn't carrying the need to fix what she didn't break. She was beginning to live in truth—and that was something I had prayed for.

Our home became quieter but not empty. Peaceful but not silent. We laughed more. We danced around the house more. I was no longer a shell of myself—I was becoming **whole** again. I learned how to say *no*. I learned how to rest. I learned how to ask for help when I needed it. And in return, my girls learned that love didn't have to come at the cost of your sanity. That being strong didn't mean staying somewhere that broke you.

My new relationship taught them something, too—not just that love could be different, but that **I** could be different. They saw affection that wasn't forced, apologies that came without excuses, and a man who didn't just take up space but added to it. For the first time, they had a front-row seat to what partnership could look like when it's rooted in care—not chaos.

These weren't just new experiences. They were corrections. They were moments that rewrote the narrative I had unknowingly passed down.

The cycle didn't end when I left. It started to break the moment I chose *peace* over pretending. And the real reward wasn't just my healing—it was giving my girls a different lens to see themselves, their worth, and their future through.

Peace Over Pretending

Looking back now, I realize that every hard decision I made, every tear I cried in silence, every moment I thought I wouldn't make it—was leading me here. To this version of myself. The one who no longer chooses pain in the name of love. The one who knows peace is not a luxury—it's a necessity. The one who understands that *legacy* isn't just what you leave behind, it's what you live out loud.

I used to think being strong meant staying. That it meant sacrificing my own happiness for the sake of a picture-perfect family. But now I know— *real strength* is *choosing yourself when everything in you has been trained not to.*

I don't regret telling my story. I don't regret walking away. And I don't regret rebuilding, even when it hurt.

Because peace over pretending isn't just a decision. It's *a declaration.*

And I hope my daughters don't just remember the woman who stayed too long...

I hope they remember the woman who finally stood up—and walked away.

CHAPTER 4

The Inheritance
I Never Meant to Give

I didn't realize just how closely my children were watching me until I saw them start to walk in shoes that looked far too familiar—shoes that resembled mine.

The first moment that truly hit me was when my oldest daughter entered a relationship with her third child's father. It was like watching a rerun of my life play out on a different stage. No matter how he treated her, she stayed. She made excuses. She carried the weight of their relationship on her back, believing that somehow, love meant surviving it—not thriving in it. I'd sit and try to talk to her—plead with her—to see things differently, to want more. But nothing I said ever stuck. It was like I was yelling into a windstorm. And deep down, I realized why—because she was doing what I had done. She wasn't listening to what I said. She was following what I lived.

It's a lot easier to analyze someone else's relationship from the outside than it is to survive your own from the inside. Watching her fall into patterns I fought so hard to break shattered me in a way I wasn't prepared for.

Then came the shift I noticed in my son. He had always been my quiet one—my introvert who kept to himself, rarely expressing his emotions. When he moved out to be with a girl he met at work and later married her, I didn't even find out about the wedding until the night it happened. I remember sitting in the hospital room with my dying grandmother when I got the news, and I just sat there in silence, holding it all in like I always did.

He was such a good-hearted young man—so giving, so loyal. But sometimes those qualities made him vulnerable. I watched people take advantage of him, just like I had watched people take advantage of me. One year, he and his wife moved back in with us in North Carolina from South Carolina, and he arranged to have some furniture returned through a family member of hers. It was never returned. That decision—one simple act of misplaced trust—ended with him being charged with a felony. And once again, I saw him carry the consequences of trying to do right by others, even at his own expense. I never wanted him to become his father, but the traits I wanted to shield him from—the ones that had quietly formed in the shadows—were already there.

I saw it in my third child, too. She rarely talked about her feelings, but her actions told the story. The days I wasn't working 16-hour shifts, she would come home from high school and go straight to sleep. On the days I was gone, she stepped into my shoes like it was second nature. She cooked, cleaned, and looked after her younger siblings without ever complaining. She became the nurturer. The strong one. She'd open the cabinets and refrigerator and somehow made magic out of nothing. To this day, people still rave about her food, telling her she should open her own restaurant. I couldn't see it then, but now I know—she had been filling my shoes far too early.

The weight of it all hit me like a flood. I felt sadness. Guilt. Shame. Frustration. A deep sense of helplessness. I had tried so many times to step in, to warn them, to guide them onto a different path—but by then, they were grown. They'd look me in the eye and say, "I'm an adult now. This isn't about how I grew up. This is my choice." And while I knew they were trying to protect me from more pain, I could feel the denial. I could see myself in them even when they couldn't.

The hardest part wasn't what I saw—it was what I couldn't change. I had passed down a blueprint I never meant to draw and watching them use it broke me.

About two years ago, one of my daughters confided in me during a tough moment. She was struggling with her relationship, and I was trying to understand why she was holding on so tightly. And then she said it: "I suffer from separation anxiety. It started when I was a child when you were never home."

She wasn't blaming me—she was just telling the truth. But her words ripped through me like a blade. I had spent all those years working, sacrificing, trying to provide a life they didn't have to recover from but somewhere in the chaos of surviving, I left cracks I never saw forming.

And that's when it hit me: I wasn't the only one trying to survive. They were, too.

I never meant for my kids to be my silent teachers—but they were. In their choices, their heartbreaks, their silence, and even in their strength, they showed me the weight of the legacy I was passing on. And that mirror changed everything.

Section 2
Their Voices: What They Carried, What They Learned

This next section holds something deeply personal: the reflections of my children—the five hearts who witnessed our home from the inside out. Some of their words are raw. Some are tender. Some are still guarded. And that's okay. Each voice carries its own weight, its own truth, and its own pace.

You'll notice that the tone shifts from story to story. Some of my children offered full reflections. Others only gave pieces. Some responded in detail. Others asked me to fill in the rest based on what I've seen and known as their mother. You'll hear them in their own words when possible—and when not, you'll hear them through mine.

These stories aren't polished or uniform. They weren't written to impress or explain. They were offered with courage and trust.

My hope is that as you read them, you'll do so with an open heart—one that honors their honesty, even when it hurts, and holds space for the complexity of growing up in a home that held both love and pain.

This section is sacred. It's theirs. And I'm honored to share it with you.

Learning to Love Without Losing Myself

I had a normal childhood growing up. I had a roof over my head, food to eat, clothes on back, and friends/family I could depend on. Growing up in a household with four other siblings was not without its challenges. So many personalities clashing consistently made you want to spend as much time away as possible. Constant fighting over who's going to sit shotgun in the car, what music to play, what to watch on the TV, almost everything else in between. No one brought out my own insecurities more than my siblings, whether they meant it as a joke or not. It was a constant battle and every time they brought it up it fueled my anxiety more and more. I was losing to my insecurities and there was nothing I could do.

My siblings had their own interests and things they did in their free time and so did I. Although we clashed a lot I loved supporting them in all their accomplishments. Growing up, I often felt like my voice or my opinion didn't matter, it was constantly overshadowed by my other siblings. I often found myself knowing the answers or wanting to speak up in school but could never form the words to speak out because deep down, I felt whatever I had to say would not matter. In some ways, that still affects the decisions I make today. I rather keep to myself and let others lead the conversation. I want to become more social and engage more with others, but my anxiety keeps me prisoner.

My parents' relationship from what I remember was average. They tried to act cordial in front of everyone and keep their arguments to themselves, but I could always tell when there was tension in the air. They didn't really do a lot of things together or show a lot of affection in public. My mom worked all the time while my dad did a bunch of construction jobs and projects. I spent a lot of time with my dad, and I knew if I had any problems I could go to him, and he wouldn't hesitate to help me.

Looking back, I wish my mom didn't have to work as much. I wish she showed up to cheer me on when it came to school events like she did my other siblings. I wish she came to me and told me how proud she was of what I was doing and how much she hated not being there instead of dismissing me. I didn't learn a lot about love from watching my parents, but I loved the relationship I had with my father. I could count on him, and he would never let me down.

That feeling of having someone you can go to, and you know for sure they will listen to your problems, talk you through solutions, and even try to put you on to other ways to look at things and handle situations is what I wanted, and it became the basis for all my relationships growing up. As I got older, I learned more about dating from shows and watching my other siblings relationships.

From them, I knew I wanted to date for marriage, and I also knew that no matter what I was going to put myself first in every relationship. I was very picky on who I gave my time to. I wanted a relationship that was healthy, fun, adventurous, epic. The few relationships I had were not always that way, but they were good all the same. Things happen where people simply grow apart, move away, or just disappear altogether.

Going into every relationship, it was important for me to know what things I would put up with and the things that I would not. Whenever there were problems I always tried to talk it out and find solutions, then give our relationship time to see if any effort had been made to improve our relationship. Sometimes it worked, sometimes it went right out the door and in the sewage.

Whenever it got to the point where I tried multiple times to find solutions and was still unhappy, I ended it. There was no point in staying. I knew the type of love I wanted, I knew what I deserved, and I knew I wasn't going to settle for anything less than. Even when it came to relationships that lasted years. I believed *love* is a choice and once you choose to stop loving me, there's no reason for me to stay.

If I could go back to talk to my younger self about love and relationships, I would let her know to give yourself some grace, be patient, and keep moving forward. Don't go searching, let it find you, and let it happen naturally. I've learned love is a choice that requires sacrifice. You are constantly choosing to love someone even through the rough patches. Every sacrifice made will come back 10-fold as blessings because it was made without hesitation and with love. I've also learned to stop blocking my blessings, there's no benefit to staying where you're not wanted, appreciated, respected, or loved. While it's easier said than done, *walking away* could just be the salvation you needed.

When it comes to love and relationships today, the two don't seem to coexist or even run in the same circle. Everyone is in a relationship but there's no love. You also see people who claim they're in love but continues to step out of their relationship and cheat. There's no accountability for one's actions but always an excuse. Though I try not to, I still find myself repeating patterns I saw with my parents when it comes to my own relationship. I can get snappy, and my facial expressions will tell you off before I do. The biggest part of my parents' relationship that unknowingly influenced mine was their communication style. *Communication* is a major issue that I still struggle with; when I'm upset or hurt, I shut down; and when I'm irritated or annoyed, I'm a little sassy with lots of smart remarks. This is something I know I have to work on for myself and to better my relationship.

As a child, we were stable but living paycheck to paycheck. Though we were "comfortable," that came at the expense of having to sacrifice spending any time with my mother. Now that I'm older, I understand the sacrifices my mom had to make to keep a roof over our heads, food on the table, and clothes on our backs. I knew that's not the type of stability I wanted. I wanted to be able to provide and still have the freedom to spend time with my family. Those values are still true today, which is why I'm often looking for better opportunities. I refuse to settle for some mediocre job that's going to drive me crazy and take me away from my family. I do a lot of things differently from what I saw growing up. I will always put my feelings first in any relationship because I know how it is to stay in a relationship that's not empowering and only drains your energy. I refuse to lose myself trying to please someone else.

This is my story. The one shaped by quiet strength and hard lessons—but defined by choosing myself, again and again.

My Reflection As Her Mother

Reading her words stirred something deep in me. I saw her strength, her honesty, and her journey to create a life that feels safe and whole. But I also felt the sting of absence—the moments I missed, the affirmations I didn't give. She didn't need perfection from me; she needed presence. And even though I can't rewrite the past, I honor her voice and her healing now. She's choosing herself in ways I wish I had. That's not just growth—that's legacy shifting right in front of my eyes.

Built From The Wreckage

Growing up in our home was very interesting. Interesting in a way where it felt like we weren't living together as a family—but more so just trying to survive as individuals. Love and relationships. From what I saw between Mom and Dad, this thing called love, this thing called marriage, it felt like just a pretty title. Beautiful words escaping your lips that didn't really mean anything. The things I witnessed didn't resemble anything I wanted to look forward to, so watching them turned me cold to a lot of potential relationships. Honestly, I feel like I'm more calloused than ever—like I refuse to let those words, "I love you," ever escape my lips again.

I've stayed in relationships even when I wasn't happy. Mom and Dad were my first example of what a relationship looked like. Watching her endure everything made me believe that walking away wasn't an option. That idea embedded itself so deeply in me that I'm still trying to unlearn it and create a healthier, more balanced way of thinking. I don't blame Mom for any of it. She did the best she could with the cards she was dealt. Everything she went through was necessary to bring her to where she is now—and I'm so proud of her.

If I could talk to my younger self, I'd tell her to be selfish with her time. Accomplish your goals and dreams first. Let that love thing come later. Because if it's costing you your peace—it's costing you too much. That's the number one lesson I've learned.

I've also come to understand that I'm still carrying a lot from the past. I've repeated patterns I saw growing up—because, honestly, you only know what you've been exposed to. But now, I know better. And I know I have to take over and change those patterns before they define me. For me, staying through everything—no matter the reason or the disrespect—was what I thought love looked like. I thought that was normal.

Trust, communication, emotional safety—all of that changed once I started experiencing trauma in my own relationship. In the beginning, I thought I had it together. But eventually, the weight of what I'd been through caught up with me. Growing up in our home might've laid the foundation, but it didn't shape everything—I've learned that shaping is a forever journey.

What I'm trying to do differently is keep toxic energy and dysfunction out of my relationships. I still believe in loving someone unconditionally—but I've learned that you have to love yourself more. That's one of the biggest things I'm still learning: how to create a healthy balance for myself in every area of life—not just romantically.

And honestly? I'm grateful for this experience. It became the foundation for me to be great. For me to teach and show my kids—and other women—that there's beauty in the pain. So, take hold of the paintbrush and paint away beautifully. Your past does not define you.

And Mom—if you're reading this, I just want to say that I am beyond proud of you. I know it's been far from easy, but you make it look effortless. You are right where you're supposed to be—even when it doesn't feel like it. My only advice for you in this moment is to remain kind. Don't allow the current or past trauma to taint your heart posture. Believe it or not, I'm actually grateful for this experience—because without it, I wouldn't be the phenomenal woman I'm continuously growing into every day.

This is my story. The one born from survival, rebuilt through truth, and defined by who I've chosen to become.

My Reflection As Her Mother

Reading her words brought tears to my eyes—not because of the pain, but because of her power. I saw pieces of myself in her, but also parts of her I wish I had at her age: her self-awareness, her courage, her refusal to stay broken. She took what was shattered and started rebuilding—carefully, intentionally, beautifully. I know I passed down some patterns I didn't mean to, but what she's doing now? That's healing the next generation. That's what breaking cycles looks like. And to hear her say, *she's proud of me,* reminds me why telling this story matters.

The Quiet One: What He Carries in Silence

My son has always been the quiet one. Even as a child, he stayed to himself— never loud, never demanding, never trying to be seen. But as his mother, I saw him. I saw the softness in him, the way he'd give you the shirt off his back or his last dollar without hesitation. His heart is big, generous, and loyal.

That softness, though, is wrapped in a tough shell. His exterior is harder now—guarded and sharp around the edges. He speaks with intensity, his words sometimes laced with frustration or hurt. But I've come to understand that it's not anger—it's armor. It's the residue of pain carried from a decade of trying to make sense of life, love, and everything in between.

He's chosen not to participate in this section. Not because he doesn't care—but because that's simply who he is - private, quiet, and often deep in thought. But over the years, in quiet conversations or in passing remarks, he's shared just enough for me to piece together the weight he carries.

He once shared that he thought marriage and love were supposed to last forever. That belief began to unravel the moment his father and I divorced. He stated that's when he realized nothing lasts forever. It shifted something in him. He also told me that the way he lived his 20s—the decisions, the relationships, the regrets—wasn't something he wanted to carry into his 30s.

That kind of self-awareness told me more than a hundred conversations ever could.

There's something sacred in the way he moves through the world—quietly, intentionally, protectively. And though he may not speak much, I've learned to hear what *isn't* said. His silence is not absence. It's a form of strength. A language only a mother truly understands.

This is for the sons who love hard, live quietly, and carry more than they'll ever say out loud. I see *you*. I see *him*. And I honor the way you heal—on your own terms.

This section is for him. The one who never needed many words to tell the truth.

My Reflection As His Mother

He may not say much, but I've always known how deeply he feels. His presence speaks louder than words ever could. Watching him grow into a man—one who questions, reflects, protects, and rebuilds in his own quiet way—has been one of my greatest honors. I don't need a long letter from him to know who he is. I've always known. And I'll always be proud of him, whether he's speaking or simply standing in his truth.

The Love I Wanted, The Hurt I Learned

For a while, it felt like everything I ever wanted. A two-parent household. Something so many of my friends had and I'd always wished for. I remember the comfort of having both Mom and Dad under the same roof, the noise of my siblings all together, the laughter, the fights, the memories. Even when we didn't always get along, I loved that time. I loved having a full house.

But I also remember the quiet tension. The kind that wrapped around the walls late at night when they thought I was sleeping. The yelling behind closed doors. The loud silence in the mornings after. They tried to shield us from it, but we knew. Thin walls don't lie.

What I saw between Mom and Dad wasn't what I wanted for myself. I didn't want to walk on eggshells. I didn't want a love that went unspoken when things got hard. I wanted clarity. Safety. Peace. But when the family started to fall apart—when my mom finally left—I didn't just lose a version of home, I lost my dad, too. His calls grew less and less. Eventually, they stopped. And the silence that followed was loud. Deafening. It felt like he didn't just divorce Mom, he divorced us, too. That loss left a gap I tried to fill.

I started seeking love in men. I got attached quickly—sometimes after just a few weeks—because I was starving for connection. For validation. For that missing fatherly love. I fell for someone who I thought saw me, who I thought could be my future. But that relationship, too, became a mirror I didn't want to look into.

It started with the cheating. Valentine's Day, of all days. I showed up to his house full of hope—greeted by gifts and balloons. But the real surprise was what I found the next morning: a used condom in the trash. My heart shattered, but I stayed. I forgave. I thought that was the worst of it—until it wasn't. Until he sat across from me one night and said the words no woman ever wants to hear: "I have an STD." I cried right there in front of him. Not just for the betrayal, but for the fact that I had to walk away from someone I thought I could build a life with.

But that wasn't even the deepest scar. What hurt just as much was the slow erosion of who I was. He was controlling so much so, that I gave up opportunities just to keep the peace. I remember being so excited about finally having a dance team at school, wanting to join the majorettes my senior year. But he shut it down. "Too short. Too revealing. I don't want anyone seeing your body." His jealousy disguised itself as love, and I let go of something that brought me joy because of it.

I started silencing myself the way I saw Mom do. And it took time to realize that it wasn't love.

Through all of this, I started to unlearn. To recognize the ways I was repeating cycles I never asked for. I learned that love should never make you lose yourself. That you don't need to stay just because someone says they love you. That just because someone apologizes, doesn't mean the pain didn't matter. I learned that stability isn't just about staying—it's about being seen, being safe, being respected.

One of the hardest moments from childhood that still sits with me is the night I wasn't supposed to be listening, but I was. I heard the commotion, stood behind my door with anger and tears, and when I finally got the courage to knock—I saw it. The abuse. I saw my mother being pushed against a wall. That night changed me. It confirmed that I never wanted that kind of love. I wanted the opposite.

I'm still learning. Still growing. Still healing. I've made different choices—quieter ones, maybe, but intentional. I've learned to walk away when I need to. I've learned not to give 100% to someone giving me 10%. I've learned to communicate even when it's hard. And I'm learning that love doesn't have to hurt. That love, real love, makes room for you to breathe.

This is my story. The one shaped by what I saw but not defined by it.

My Reflection As Her Mother

Reading her story cracked something open in me. Not because I didn't know it—but because hearing it in her words reminded me how much she carried silently. I never wanted her to model her love after mine. I never wanted her to give up her voice to feel worthy. And yet, I see the moments where she did. And I also see the strength it took to come back from it.

She's rewriting the narrative—not by pretending it didn't happen, but by choosing to rise in spite of it. Her pain was real. Her heartbreak was real. But so is her healing. And that's what makes me proud beyond words.

The Mirror I Didn't Mean To Hold

Dear Mom,

Growing up in our home was a rollercoaster. I remember my dad having to step up and be the mother and father of the house while we supported you in nursing school to become the best nurse you could be.

Watching you stay in your relationship for so long made me feel like whenever I had children, I would not treat them differently. As a child, I thought about living to become an adult, but as I got older, I started to realize God has the final say so.

When it came to love and relationships, I learned that no matter how hard your relationship gets, you never give up—from watching you and Dad. Because of that, I now know that both parties have their own feelings and have to learn each other in my own relationships.

There were times when I wished I could have a reset in life. But if I could go back and tell my younger self something about our family, I would say, "Please, Mom and Dad, stop fighting and work together and love one another."

Today, I see things differently because I am my parents' child. I have learned that you only have one life to live. Even though things weren't perfect, I want you to know I'm glad I'm the woman that I am today.

Love, J1

A Mother's Note

Of all my children, my oldest daughter's journey has mirrored mine the most. She carries a strength I admire and a resilience I recognize—because I've lived it, too. When I asked her to share her reflections, she gave me what she could. Her words—what she did share—are included here exactly as she wrote them.

But there was more I've seen. More I've carried as her mother. And since she didn't get a chance to finish the second half of the questionnaire, I've filled in the rest with what I know to be true—through observation, through late-night conversations, through the heart of a mother who sees her child even when they think they're hiding.

It's not a perfect story—but none of ours are. It's honest. It's hers. And I'm honored to share it.

My oldest daughter has always been the one who mirrored me the most—her sacrifices, her strength, even her silence. And though her letter is brief, every word carries weight. I know she's busy raising five children of her own, helping with two more of her partner's kids, and even watching a friend's child on top of juggling two or three jobs. So when she says she doesn't have time to answer the second part, I understand. But as her mother, I've seen the parts she didn't write down.

She may say she's in a better place now—and I pray that's true—but I've watched her minimize her pain the way I once did. I've heard her say she's fine, even when her eyes said otherwise. I've offered for her to come home, to take a break, to reset—but she carries her life the way I carried mine: all at once, and often alone.

Her relationship reminds me of mine in ways that ache. The emotional weight. The lack of help. A partner who refuses to watch the kids while she works long hours. The pieces may not match exactly, but the patterns—they echo. She's living a life I recognize too well, and it's heartbreaking, because I know how that story feels.

And yet, what breaks me even more is knowing she learned it from me. Not intentionally—but by watching me stay too long. Watching me fight for love while losing pieces of myself. She saw me endure, and she thought that was strength. I wanted to teach resilience—but I taught survival. I wanted to show love—but I showed sacrifice. I wanted better for her, and instead, she inherited the very burden I tried to protect her from.

This is the hardest mirror to look into—the one where I see myself reflected in her choices, her struggles, her silence. The one I didn't mean to pass down. But even still, I believe in her healing. I believe her story is still being written, just like mine was. And I pray that one day, she'll choose herself sooner than I did.

This is her story—and mine. A story shaped by what we lived, what we carried, and what we're still unlearning.

My Reflection As Her Mother

Of all my children's voices, hers was the hardest to read—and the most familiar. Because in her, I saw me. Not just the woman I was, but the girl I used to be. The one who wanted love so deeply, she mistook pain for purpose. The one who stayed, hoping her sacrifice was enough. My daughter carries so much, and though her words were few, her story is not. I know the weight she holds. I know where she got it. And I know now it's my job—not to fix it—but to own it, speak it, and pray that one day she'll release what I never meant to pass down. This is the hardest mirror, but it's also the most important one to face.

I asked my children to share their voices, not just for the sake of this book, but for the sake of truth—for the sake of healing. Each of their reflections offered something different: pain, clarity, strength, and silence.

But woven through all of them was one common thread—they were watching *me*, even when I didn't know they were. They learned love by watching me hold it. They learned pain by watching me endure it. And while I didn't intend to pass on those patterns, I see now that I did.

That's where we go next. Into the hardest part of all: The inheritance I never meant to give.

Section 3
What My Staying Taught Them

The moments I really started connecting the dots—between my choices and the emotional patterns I was seeing in my children—began when my oldest daughter started juggling three or four jobs as a CNA. She was doing everything she could to keep the lights on, provide a roof over their heads, and maintain a home with her partner at the time. Despite how difficult and unbalanced that relationship was, she stayed. And I saw myself all over again. I couldn't help but think, *She's staying for all the wrong reasons—trying to give her kids what she thinks they need: a father in the home.*

As for my son, I didn't realize how deeply he'd been affected until much later. By the time the divorce happened, he had already moved out, gotten married, and was living with his wife's family. For the longest time, I thought he had a stronger bond with his father than he did with me. He never questioned his dad's absence or inconsistencies. But me? The moment I started moving forward—when I eventually remarried—he had questions. That's when I saw the double standard. And it hurt. I realized that, in his eyes, I'd always been the strong one. Maybe he didn't see my pain—just my duty.

My third child, my middle daughter, was another reflection. No matter how many times her children's father left or let her down, she took him back.

Even when he walked away for other women—and she knew it—she stayed. I'll never forget the time, when her baby was barely one, he took the crib and gave it to someone else. That moment still sits heavy in my chest. It was the first time I saw her clearly walking a path that looked far too much like mine.

But my two youngest daughters? Their outlook seemed different. They were raised in the same house, but somehow came out with different views on love, on relationships, and on themselves. That difference both relieved and puzzled me. How could five kids grow up in the same home and turn out so different?

When I reflect on the unhealthy attachments I witnessed in my older children, the list is long—and painful. Fights. Screaming. Things thrown. Being shot at while the kids were in the car. Depression. Drinking. Replacing love with relationships that drained them. They weren't looking for chaos. They were looking for comfort—for familiarity. Even if that familiarity was broken. And that familiar? That came from me. That truth is one of the hardest to live with.

I'll never forget watching my daughter walk in after another long shift, only to see her partner give nothing back. Or my son going to jail for something he didn't do—because of loyalty. Or hearing one of my girls say, "I suffer from separation anxiety," and trace it back to when I was never home. That comment nearly split me in half.

I worked so much because I thought that's what being a good mother meant—making sure they had what I didn't. But I never considered the price they'd pay in my absence. The time I thought I was giving them a better life, I was also giving them wounds I didn't see until it was too late. And that's where the mom's guilt screams the loudest.

I thought I was doing right. I thought I was protecting them. But in the end, they picked up habits and heartaches from what I modeled—not what I said.

I believe they understand now. Even my two youngest, who have their own opinions about how I raised their older siblings, can now see why I stayed—and why I eventually left. I try to be transparent with all of them. If they ask, I answer. I don't sugarcoat anymore. I tell the truth. Because hiding it never protected them. It only delayed the healing.

I still feel emotionally tied to each of them in a way that's hard to explain. Even though they're grown, I still want to protect them. I still feel like I'm making up for lost time. And sometimes, I wonder—am I doing too much? Am I being overprotective? But that's what happens when you've been the mother, the father, the provider, the peacekeeper, the everything.

One thing I've learned and want other mothers to know:

Don't stay just for the kids. Not unless staying comes with love, healing, and growth. Don't mistake presence for protection. Have the hard conversations. Be honest—with yourself and with them.

Because what they see becomes what they repeat. And what we don't heal becomes what they inherit.

The Cost They Inherited

I never meant to hand my children pain wrapped in love. I never meant to teach them how to stay when I should've shown them how to walk away. I meant to give them stability, protection, and a better life than I had. But now I see it all so clearly—how my silence shaped their voices, how my endurance shaped their expectations, how my choices became their blueprint. And while I can't rewrite what they saw, I can tell the truth about it. I can name the patterns. I can own what I passed down. Because healing doesn't come from pretending it didn't happen—it comes from choosing differently. And that choice starts now.

CHAPTER 5
The Healing That Followed

For so long, I said, "I never wanted to be like my mom or dad. I didn't want to have kids by different men like my father, whom had different kids by different women, and I didn't want men coming in and out of my life like my mother." I wanted one man. One family. One home. That dream—simple and sacred—held me hostage for over 25 years. I clung to it through the cheating, the abuse, the loneliness. I stayed because I believed my children deserved the image of a whole family.

But the day I stepped outside of my marriage—emotionally and physically—that was the day I knew I was no longer the woman who stayed.

Even during past separations, I never truly allowed myself to move on. Some part of me always believed I'd go back. That belief had woven itself into my identity. So when I gave even a small piece of myself to someone else, it wasn't just an act—it was a release. A silent, powerful breaking of the chain. That was the moment I let go emotionally, even if the legal divorce came later. Something in me had shifted. And I knew—I wasn't going back.

And yet, even after the divorce papers were signed, I didn't feel free. I still felt like I had to answer to him. For over two decades, that had been my role—his wife, his mirror, his shadow. And survival habits don't fall away just because a judge stamps a signature. For nearly a year and a half, I still felt like a prisoner. I moved in silence. I looked over my shoulder. Even relocating to another state didn't bring peace—not right away. The peace came only after I moved back to North Carolina and put distance not just in miles, but in mindset.

That season after the divorce wasn't a celebration. It was quiet. Almost too quiet. I wasn't grieving the man—I had grieved him long ago. I was grieving the dream. The little girl in me who wanted to be like her aunt. The teenager who said, "I'll do it differently than my parents." The mother who stayed, not for herself, but for five little hearts who didn't ask to be born into chaos. I was saying goodbye to the picture I once painted of a "normal" family. And that goodbye? It was harder than I expected.

One of the biggest shifts I experienced was rediscovering my worth. After years of being silenced—of having no voice, of being dismissed and gaslit—I had forgotten what it felt like to speak without fear. Even now, in my marriage, I'm still learning how to have hard conversations. I still catch myself holding back, afraid I'll spark an argument. But the difference now? I know I deserve to be heard. And that's a truth I'm learning to lean into.

Freedom didn't come in a wave—it came in layers. At first, it felt foreign. Like I didn't deserve it. There were times I hid my new partner from my ex, even though we were divorced. Times I tiptoed, still trying to protect everyone from fallout. But eventually, I found peace in the ordinary—in quiet mornings, in laughter with my daughters, in a home that didn't feel like a battleground.

Freedom came slowly. But when it did, it felt like breathing after holding it in for years.

Still, the guilt lingered. Guilt over the years I lost. Guilt over what my children saw. Guilt over what they carried because of what I allowed. But I remind myself daily—guilt is not the same as responsibility. I did what I thought was right at the time, even when it cost me parts of myself. And now,

I get to teach my children a new lesson: how to choose yourself. How to heal. How to walk away from what hurts, even when it once felt like home.

If I could sit beside the younger me—the girl who met him at sixteen— I'd hold her hand and whisper:

You are loved. You are worthy. You are more than what he sees in you. You don't have to earn someone's love by enduring their pain. You can walk away. And you will. Because the day I chose me wasn't just about leaving him. It was about returning to myself.

Section 2
The Daughters My Healing Raised

There's a kind of healing that doesn't just transform you—it transforms everything you touch, especially your children. And for me, the clearest evidence of that healing lives in my two youngest daughters. They were raised by a different version of me. Not perfect. Not fully healed. But freer. Wiser. More whole than the woman who raised their older siblings.

Unlike their siblings, my youngest girls weren't raised entirely in survival mode—but they still witnessed more than I wish they had. They heard the fights. They felt the tension. By the time I filed for divorce, they were 15 and 11. My youngest, although old enough to remember some things, doesn't carry the full weight of what we went through—and honestly, I thank God for that.

Because by the time they were stepping into adolescence, I had already begun choosing myself. I had started breaking the patterns. I was learning how to set boundaries, how to speak up, and how to protect my peace. And in choosing myself, I was finally able to choose them more fully, too—not just as their provider, but as a present, emotionally safe mother.

Their relationship with love looks completely different. They don't stay where they're not valued. They don't accept *bare-minimum energy* just to say they have someone. *Red flags* are what they are—and they walk away when their peace is disturbed. And the most beautiful part? They do it without guilt.

I've watched them chase their futures boldly. College. Career paths. Dreams that weren't wrapped around a man or defined by someone else's love. My fourth daughter graduated with her bachelor's degree in business. My youngest is working toward her degree in criminal justice. They wanted more. They worked for more. And most importantly—they believed they deserved more.

When my fourth daughter got her license, I didn't have the money to buy her a car. But I handed her mine. She drove it for a year, worked hard, and eventually bought her own car outright—no payments. My baby girl did the same. She used one of my cars, saved her money, and by the time she turned 18, she had her own vehicle, too. Watching their independence unfold was like seeing living proof that the cycle had really been broken. But that doesn't mean there weren't hard moments.

There were moments that still ache. Like seeing my youngest cry silently when her father didn't show up for her graduation—after he had traveled for her sister's. Or hearing her say, in complete numbness, "It is what it is," when I asked how she felt about their relationship. That was hard. But it was real. And it reminded me that healing often requires distance—even from the people we once needed most.

The beauty, though, is that both of them know their worth. They know love should feel safe—not heavy. That partnership should uplift—not consume. They learned what not to accept not just by watching my pain— but by watching *my shift*. By seeing the difference once I finally chose myself.

That's what I carry with me now—the quiet confidence that even though I can't rewrite the past, I got to rewrite the ending. And in doing so, I helped shape a different beginning for them. They are the daughters my healing raised.

And to my oldest three children—I need you to know something from the depths of my heart...

I am so sorry that I stayed too long. I'm sorry you didn't get the version of me that your younger sisters did. You deserved her, too.

Where Healing Begins

And while I can't go back and give my oldest children the version of me I became—I can love them with the wisdom I've gained. I can show up for them now, with softness and truth. I can be a safe place, even if I wasn't always a perfect one.

That's the thing about healing—it doesn't erase what happened, but it teaches you how to show up differently going forward.

And one of the hardest lessons I had to learn on this journey was forgiveness. Forgiveness is not for the other person, it's for *you*.

Not the kind that excuses someone's behavior—but the kind that frees you from carrying it.

My kids had seen so much. They had lived through the ugly side of family—anger, silence, and broken trust. And I wanted them to also see the beautiful side—growth, grace, and redemption.

One day, while in Atlanta with my youngest two daughters, I met up with my oldest daughter. I gathered them together. Their father stood nearby, and my other two children were on the phone. And in that moment, I spoke three words I never thought I'd say:

"I forgive you."

And without hesitation, he responded, "I forgive you, too, and it was my fault."

That moment didn't change the past—but it changed something in me. It loosened the grip of resentment. It let light in. And in that moment, I knew my healing had come full circle.

Because healing after staying too long is its own kind of beginning.

CHAPTER 6
The Aftermath—Healing & Lessons

I thought the healing would start the moment I signed those divorce papers. I really did.

I thought that walking away—choosing me—would bring instant freedom from everything I had endured for 25 years. But healing doesn't work like that. It's not loud. It's not sudden. It's not always visible. Healing is slow. Quiet. Layered.

I had to learn that just like pain builds over time, so does healing. You can't just say, "I'm free," and suddenly be free. It took years. And to be honest, even as I write this book, I'm still healing.

I've made incredible progress—I'm not who I was. But I'm also not yet fully who I'm becoming.

There are still moments when I catch myself holding my tongue—not because anyone's telling me to be quiet, but because I'm still unlearning the silence I once lived in. Even in my current marriage—a loving, healthy one— I sometimes hesitate to speak my truth. That fear of conflict, of being misunderstood, still lingers. But I'm working through it, day by day.

So, when I tell another woman, "You don't need a man to define you," I'm not speaking from bitterness, I'm speaking from experience. Yes, I'm remarried now- but the most important relationship in my life is the one I have with God and myself.

One of the biggest lessons I've learned is the importance of teaching your children to value their own voice. If I could go back, I would've had more intentional conversations—not just answering their questions but initiating the ones that matter. Conversations about love. About worth. About red flags and what they mean. About the truth that love should never cost your peace.

Now, with my grandchildren, I try to be that soft place to land. We may not live in the same state, and I don't see them as often as I'd like, but when we do connect—I make sure they know I'm here. I listen. I encourage. I remind them they can come to me about anything. I remind them they are deeply loved.

With my grown kids, I've had to learn to meet them where they are. They've told me, "Mom, our choices are based on our experiences, not just how we were raised." And even though I sometimes want to pour all my wisdom into them, I've learned when to step back. I've gone from being the mother who tries to fix everything—to the mother who coaches, who supports, who listens.

Yes, there's guilt. Guilt about the time I can't get back. Guilt about the days I worked 16-hour shifts while they needed me home. Guilt about staying too long and teaching them that dysfunction was normal. But guilt doesn't lead anymore.

I've apologized. I've been transparent. And now, I show up differently. Not perfectly—but presently. To the woman still stuck in the storm—still hoping, still afraid—I want you to hear this:

You don't need anyone else to validate you. You are *enough*. You are worthy of love that doesn't hurt. Of peace that isn't conditional. Of a life

that feels like yours. Don't stay "for the kids." I did that, and it cost *me*. It cost *them*.

I didn't know then what I know now: Choosing yourself is the first step toward real peace. And if you're still in the process, give yourself grace.

Healing doesn't happen all at once. You don't have to see the whole staircase—just take the first step. It's messy. It's sacred. And it's yours. When you reach that place of peace—and you will—you'll look back and realize every tear, every shift, every hard decision was worth it.

Now, I teach my children—and even my grandkids—this:

Love should never hurt. Peace is non-negotiable. And choosing yourself is not selfish. Sometimes, the bravest thing you'll ever do is walk away—and keep walking. And never look back.

I'm still learning. Still unlearning. Still discovering what it means to truly love myself. But I'm proud of who I'm becoming—even if I carry a few scars. Because those scars? They're proof. Proof that I survived. That I kept going. That I finally chose me.

Section 2
Helping Them Heal

Once I started learning how to show up for myself, I realized I also had to show up for my children in new ways. Not as the mother who did it all, held it all, and carried it all—but as a woman who could say, "I didn't get everything right. But I'm here now. And I want to do better."

Even now, there are moments when I look at them and see pieces of myself—both the healed parts and the hurting ones. And if I'm being honest, that still stings. There are wounds I unintentionally passed down. Some of them showed up in their relationships. Others lived quietly in their silence. I can't erase those moments. But I can own them. And I can be the kind of mother who holds space for the conversations I once avoided.

I've told all five of my children: "If you ever need to ask me anything, ask. If you need to say something hard, say it. You won't break me." I say it because I mean it—and because I didn't always feel like I had that freedom growing up. I didn't want to raise kids who only saw me sacrificing and surviving. I wanted them to see me becoming.

With my grandkids, I pour in what I now know: that they are loved, valued, and worthy of respect. I remind them that they can come to me with anything—even if we live in different states. I may not have always had the language back then, but I have it now—and I'm using it every chance I get.

With my grown children, the conversations are deeper. I show up differently. I ask the hard questions. I don't try to mother them with guilt or control—I mother them with honesty and compassion. They may not always want to hear it, and they may remind me that their choices are their own now. And I respect that. But I still speak, because silence created too much confusion for far too long.

There are still pieces of guilt I carry—not being as present as I wanted to be, not always having the time to just sit and talk, not being able to shield them from the things they saw or felt. But I don't run from that guilt. I speak it out loud. I say I'm sorry. I remind them that I was doing the best I could with what I knew—and I'm still learning, still growing.

If I've learned anything, it's that healing isn't just something we do for ourselves—it's something we model. My children are still watching me. Not just as their mother, but as a woman becoming. A woman who chose herself. Who now chooses truth. Who now chooses softness. Who now chooses strength. I don't need to be perfect. I just need to be present.

And to every mother still trying to love her children better while healing herself, let me say this: It's never too late to try again. The conversations might be hard. The past may still ache. But there is beauty in showing up different. There is power in showing up whole.

Section 3
Turning Pain Into Purpose

I used to believe that once the divorce was final, the story was over. That I could close the chapter, walk away, and never look back. But healing doesn't come from signed papers. Healing comes when you stop surviving—and start living. When you stop hiding your story—and finally decide to tell it.

By the time I divorced my ex-husband, my three oldest children were already grown and had families of their own—except for my son, who was married. I was still raising my two youngest daughters—one in high school and the other in middle school. I thought I had shielded them from the worst of it. I thought my silence had protected them. I smiled through the pain, held the house together with bare hands, convinced myself I was doing the right thing.

But silence is its own kind of storm. The more I tried to hold everything up, the more pieces of me fell away.

For years, I never shared the full truth about what I endured. Only a few close loved ones knew. The rest I kept tucked behind my roles—mother, nurse, wife, the woman who always "had it together." But the truth was heavy. And carrying it alone began to break something inside me.

Eventually, I realized this story wasn't just mine. It belonged to every woman who stayed too long, hoping love would be enough. To every mother who thought she was protecting her kids—only to watch them carry the very pain she tried to shield them from.

I stayed because I wanted to give them what I never had: a father in the home. A family that looked whole. But in doing so, I unknowingly handed them an inheritance of a different kind.

It took hearing my daughter say she suffers from separation anxiety—something she traced back to childhood, to me never being home because I was always working. It took my son reflecting on how he wasted his 20s and didn't want to repeat the same mistakes in his 30s. It took a random moment, driving to class, when a song came on the radio—one about wasting years on someone who didn't deserve you. And that song hit me like a memory I couldn't run from. It was my story. My children's story. A mirror I didn't expect.

And when I look at my oldest daughter—her choices, her exhaustion, her heartbreak—it feels like I'm staring into a younger version of myself. That's what hurts the most. Realizing the cycle didn't stop with me—it started again in them. That's when I knew I had to tell the truth.

Not just for me—but for them. For every woman who thinks she's *the only one*. For every daughter who becomes her mother without realizing it. For every son who mistakes endurance for love. For every child raised in a home where silence was louder than words.

I didn't start on a big stage or in a coaching program. I started right where I was—sharing bits of my truth in journal entries, quiet conversations, and unspoken prayers. I spoke up—not because I had all the answers, but because I was tired of carrying the weight alone.

I'm not leading workshops or coaching other women yet—but I know this book, these pages, this story, it matters. And maybe that's how purpose begins—not loud or perfect, but honest. Real. Purpose is born in the places that hurt the most—not in spite of the pain, but because of it.

Now, when I share my story, it's not about shame. It's about survival. It's about reclaiming power. It's about breaking the silence, so the next generation doesn't repeat the pattern. It's about redefining what love, family, and freedom can actually look like.

It took me over 25 years to walk away. But it's taken me even longer to walk fully into who I am now. A woman still healing. A woman still learning. A woman no longer afraid of her own voice. And if you're reading this, I want you to know something: Your voice matters, too.

What's Still Unfolding

For most of my life, I believed staying quiet was a form of protection. That if I just held it all together, smiled through the pain, and stayed strong, I could keep my family whole. But silence doesn't protect—it delays healing. And the moment I started telling the truth—my truth—was the moment real healing began.

Sharing this story hasn't been easy. It's required me to peel back layers I once buried, to revisit pain I tried to forget, and to stand fully in my own becoming. But what I've learned is this: Telling your story won't undo the past, but it can absolutely change the future. For you. For your children. For generations to come.

This chapter may be closing, but the healing continues. And now, I no longer walk in shame—I walk in truth.

CONCLUSION

Choosing Yourself Isn't Selfish

If there's one thing I've learned after all the years I spent holding on, it's this: Choosing yourself isn't selfish—it's survival. It's healing. It's hope.

For the longest time, I believed that staying was strength. That enduring was love. That sacrificing myself was how I proved I was a good mother. A good woman. But now I know—the strongest thing you can do sometimes is **let go**. Not just of a person, but of the version of you that believed pain was the price of love.

This story isn't just about what I survived—it's about who I became. It's about the freedom I found, the peace I claimed, and the woman who had been buried under years of silence and survival finally rising.

I've made peace with the fact that I stayed too long. But I've also made peace with the version of me who endured—because she got me here. I no longer carry shame, just lessons. I no longer shrink—I stand. And I stand for every woman who's ever asked, "Am I enough?" For every mother who thought she had to choose between her kids and herself. You don't.

You can choose you—and still be a good mother. A good woman. A whole, healed human being. You can start over at any moment. You can break cycles and build new ones. You can heal out loud. You can teach your children that love shouldn't hurt, and peace is not a privilege—it's a right.

And let me tell you something I wish someone had told me years ago: *No one is going to love you more than you.* No one is going to take care of you better than you. That kind of deep, *intentional* love, the kind that nourishes your spirit and protects your peace starts within.

So, if you're still in it—still questioning, still waiting for a sign—let this be it. You are *worthy* of the life you've been afraid to imagine. And even if it takes time, even if it's messy, even if it costs you everything. **Choosing yourself will always be worth it.**

Final Personal Note From the Author

If you've made it to this point, I just want to say—thank you. Not just for reading my story, but for holding space for your own. I didn't write this book as someone who has it all figured out. I wrote it as a mother who stayed too long, who tried too hard, and who hurt in ways I never meant to—but who is still healing, still learning, and still rising.

This isn't just a story about a woman who left. It's about a woman who found herself.

A woman who finally said, "I choose me."

If you've been holding on to something that's breaking you—whether it's a person, a pattern, or a dream that no longer fits—I hope you'll take one small step toward freedom. Maybe that step is telling the truth. Maybe it's asking for help. Maybe it's choosing peace, even if your voice shakes. I don't know what your journey looks like—but I do know this: *You don't have to carry it alone. You are worthy. You are not broken. You are allowed to let go.* And just like I'm still learning to love the woman I've become— You can learn to love the one you're becoming, too.

With love and truth,

Jacqueline Moss

Scripture

"I will restore to you the years that the locust hath eaten..."
— Joel 2:25

Final Quote

"Sometimes the bravest thing a woman can do is walk away—and never look back."

About The Author

Jacqueline Moss is a wife, mother of five, and proud Me maw. She also has a grand-dog named Bruno, who stole her heart. She's also a registered nurse and powerhouse educator with over 20 years of experience in healthcare. Armed with a master's degree in nursing education and the heart of a nurturer. She is the CEO of Angelic Heart Healthcare Solutions PLLC, a healthcare education business that trains certified professionals in lifesaving skills and career advancement. As the CEO of Angelic Heart Healthcare Solutions, Jacqueline brings passion and purpose to every lesson she shares—especially the hard ones that life has taught her.

In *When Staying Hurts*, she bares her soul to empower others to break free from toxic cycles, choose themselves, and rewrite their stories—no matter how long they've been holding on. Through her words, she reveals the emotional cost of staying too long and the strength it takes to finally walk away.

Acknowledgements

To God—my anchor, my healer, my redeemer. You never left me, even when I couldn't see a way out. Every page of this story bears witness to Your grace.

To my five children—thank you for being my greatest teachers. I see now that even in the midst of my pain, your love gave me a reason to keep going. You've each carried pieces of my story, and through your strength, I've found mine. I pray that my healing helps lighten the load you've carried for so long.

To my grandchildren, you are my heartbeat. May you grow up knowing that your worth is not tied to anyone's approval, and that peace is your birthright. I'll always be your safe place, your soft landing, and your loudest cheerleader.

To my sisters, my friends, and the women who stood in the gap when I was too tired to stand on my own, thank you for being the light I didn't even know I needed.

And to the readers of this book—whether you've lived this story or simply loved someone who has, I thank you for holding space for this truth. May it inspire your own healing, your own strength, and your own fresh start.